Editor
Erica N. Russikoff, M.A.

Editor in Chief
Karen J. Goldfluss, M.S. Ed.

Creative Director
Sarah M. Fournier

Cover Artist
Barb Lorseyedi

Illustrator
Donna Bizjack

Art Coordinator
Renée Mc Elwee

Imaging
Craig Gunnell

Publisher

Mary D. Smith, M.S. Ed.

- Contains fiction and nonfiction passages on a variety of topics
- Includes critical-thinking questions to improve comprehension
- Extends the reading by using interactive writing activities
- Correlated to the Common Core State Standards

Teacher Created Resources

Author
Susan Mackey Collins, M. Ed.

CORRELATED TO COMMON CORE STANDARDS

For correlations to the Common Core State Standards, see pages 143–144. Correlations can also be found at *http://www.teachercreated.com/standards.*

Teacher Created Resources
6421 Industry Way
Westminster, CA 92683
www.teachercreated.com

ISBN: 978-1-4206-3893-6

© *2015 Teacher Created Resources*
Made in U.S.A.

Teacher Created Resources

Table of Contents

Table of Contents *(cont.)*

Introduction

Making connections is an important part of everyday life. People strive daily to make connections with other people, events, and experiences. Making connections plays an important role in nearly everything one does. It is not surprising then that this skill must also be used in developing great readers.

Connections are vital in developing fluency in reading and in understanding a variety of texts. *Nonfiction & Fiction Paired Texts* helps emergent readers learn to make connections with both fiction and nonfiction texts. The activities in this book also help fluent readers to enhance and increase their developing reading skills. *Nonfiction & Fiction Paired Texts* is the perfect reading tool for all levels of readers.

The high-interest texts in *Nonfiction & Fiction Paired Texts* contain both fiction and nonfiction passages. The units are written in pairs that share a common idea or theme. The first passage in each unit is fiction. A nonfiction text follows each fiction story. Subjects in each unit are varied, providing a multitude of topics to engage the various interests of the readers. Topics are also age-appropriate and will appeal to children in the corresponding grade level. While reading the texts, students are encouraged to look for specific meanings and to make logical inferences from what is read.

Each unit in *Nonfiction & Fiction Paired Texts* has five pages. The texts in each set are followed by two assessment pages that contain multiple-choice questions and short-answer writing activities. These pages are designed to meet the rigor demanded by the Common Core State Standards. Each assessment leads students to look for and generally cite textual evidence when answering questions. A third page in the assessment section of each unit includes longer writing activities. The writing activities for each unit are tied to higher-order thinking and questioning skills. The writing ideas are designed to help assess a student's ability to respond to a written prompt while incorporating the skills of excellent writing.

Nonfiction & Fiction Paired Texts was written to help students gain important reading skills and practice responding to questions based on the Common Core State Standards. The different units provide practice with a multitude of standards and skills, including but not limited to the following:

- making and understanding connections between content-rich reading materials

- building reading-comprehension skills

- analyzing, comparing, and contrasting fiction and nonfiction texts

- sequencing and summarizing

- experience with text-based, multiple-choice questions

- practice with short-answer responses

- practice in developing written responses to various prompts

- understanding the genres of fiction and nonfiction texts

- quoting from texts to complete assessments

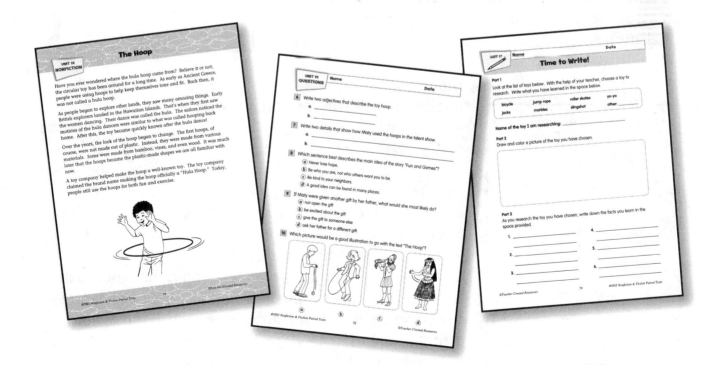

How to Use This Book

Nonfiction & Fiction Paired Texts is divided into twenty-six units. Each unit has five pages. The first two pages are texts that share a common topic or theme. Each unit contains both a fiction and nonfiction selection, as well as three assessment pages.

The book is designed so that each unit can be used separately. The activities can be completed in order, starting with the first unit and working through unit twenty-six, or they can be completed in random order. Anyone using the book may want to look for common themes or ideas that correspond with other units being taught in other subject areas. The units in this book can be used to help teach across the curriculum and to easily tie in reading and writing skills to other areas of study.

Provided with each set of fiction and nonfiction stories are three pages of assessment activities. Two of the three pages are multiple-choice and short-answer questions, which rely heavily on text-based answers. The last page in each unit is a writing page. The teacher may choose to use all three pages after completion of the connected texts, or he or she may choose to only use specific pages for assessment. Pages can be done during regular academic hours or be sent home for extra practice. Students may work on assignments alone or work with partners or in small groups.

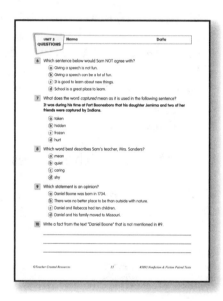

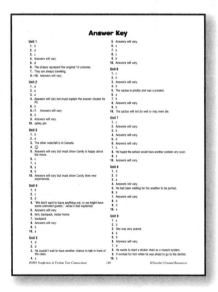

Looking at the answer key, one will notice that not all questions have answers. Many questions require short answers, which can vary, as long as the answers are based on the text. The Common Core State Standards require students to support their answer choices with information from texts, not personal opinions. Completion of the short-answer questions gives students the opportunity to practice writing their answers using information from what they have read in each unit. Of course, creativity is an equally important learning tool and is not ignored in these units. Students are given opportunities to express their own ideas and thoughts, especially in the Time to Write! activities. The writing activities are tied to the texts but are geared to give students the chance to practice the skills needed to be successful writers.

In grading the short-answer questions, teachers must verify that the answers are included in the text. Assessing the responses in the Time to Write! section is up to the teacher's discretion. Each teacher knows the abilities of the individual students in his or her class. Answers provided at one point in the year may be considered satisfactory; however, as the year progresses, the teacher's expectations of the student's writing skills will have greatly increased. A student would eventually be expected to provide better-developed responses and written work with fewer mistakes. A good idea is to keep a folder with samples of the student's work from different times during the academic year. Teachers, parents, and students can easily see progress made with the skills necessary for good writing by comparing samples from earlier in the year to the student's present writing samples.

The units in *Nonfiction & Fiction Paired Texts* can also be used to help students understand the basic principles of text. One way to do this is to teach students to use a specific reading method. Students can use the UNC method (see pages 8–9) to help gain a better understanding of how text is presented on the page and to develop and refine skills for reading for detail. After the UNC method is mastered, students will learn to automatically employ these skills in their everyday reading without having to be coached to complete the process. The skills of good reading will become automatic.

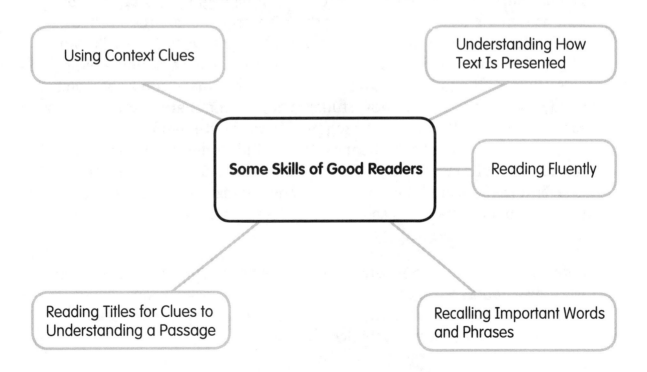

Using Context Clues

Understanding How Text Is Presented

Some Skills of Good Readers

Reading Fluently

Reading Titles for Clues to Understanding a Passage

Recalling Important Words and Phrases

Understanding and Using the UNC Method

U Underline and read all titles.

N Place numbers by all the paragraphs.

C Put circles around or highlight all important words and phrases in the text.

When students are presented with a text, they can use the UNC method to help break down the material. Students immediately underline and read all titles. To better manage the material, students next add a number beside each paragraph. This helps teachers as they go over questions. They can easily ask the students to look at a specific paragraph to point out information that helped to answer a particular question. Using this method, teachers may also discover there are students who have simply not learned how to tell where a paragraph begins or ends. This explains why many times when a teacher asks a student to read a specific paragraph, he or she cannot. The student may honestly be unsure of where to start!

The final step in the UNC method is to circle or highlight important words or phrases in the text. By completing this step, students are required to read for detail. At first, the teacher may find that many students will want to highlight entire paragraphs. Teachers will want to use a sample unit to guide students through the third step. Teachers can make copies of a unit already highlighted to help show students how to complete the third step. Teachers can work through a unit together with the students, or they may even want to use a document camera so the students can easily see the process as they work on a unit together in class. Students will soon discover that there are important details and context clues that can be used to help understand which information is the most important in any given text.

Students need to have confidence in their abilities to succeed at any given task. This is where the UNC method is a bonus in any classroom. When using this method, students can be successful in reading any text and answering the questions that follow.

The UNC method is especially helpful in aiding students to carefully read new or unfamiliar texts. Highlighters are helpful when working with printed texts but are not necessary. (For example, students can use different highlighter colors to complete each step.) Students who consistently use this method will eventually no longer need to physically highlight or circle the text as the necessary skills to great reading become an automatic response with any text. Students who consistently practice the UNC method make mental maps of what they have read and often no longer need to look back at the text when answering the questions! The UNC method allows students who are kinesthetic learners to have a physical activity that can take place during a reading activity. Visual learners are greatly aided by this method, as well. Students are encouraged by their positive progress and look forward to the challenge of reading a new text.

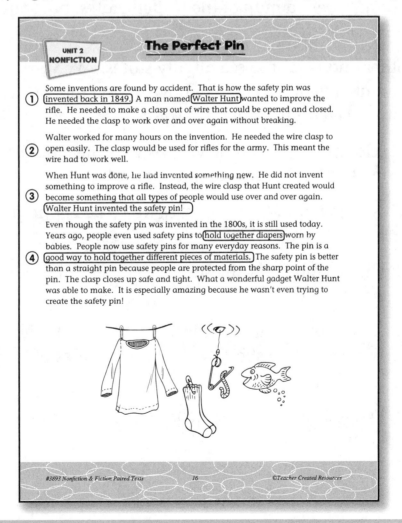

Home on Wheels

Lana liked her grandparents' house. She couldn't visit them as much as she wanted. Her grandparents' house was on wheels! They lived in a motor home. They did not stay at a house on land. Instead, they lived in their motor home. They traveled all around the country. When they came to visit, they would park their house in Lana's parents' driveway. They always seemed so happy to see Lana and her parents. Lana wished they would never go away, but she knew how much they loved to travel.

"Grandpa," Lana asked her grandfather one day when he was home for a visit, "why do you and Grandmother travel so much?"

Instead of explaining, Lana's grandfather walked her over to the kitchen. He told her to take a look at all the magnets on the front of the refrigerator. She could tell the magnets were a map of the United States, but some of the states were missing.

"Your grandmother and I want to see all fifty states. We want to learn everything we can about each state. We have eleven more states to visit before we can say we have seen all the states in America."

"I get it!" Lana exclaimed. "Each time you visit a state, you get a magnet. You are making a map of all the places you have seen."

"That's right. This map reminds us of places we've been and places we still want to see."

Lana sighed. She understood, but she still missed her grandparents. "I miss you when you are gone," Lana said.

"We miss you, too." Her grandfather walked her around to the side of the refrigerator. Lana smiled when she saw so many pictures of herself mounted to the side.

"Well," Lana said with a smile, "I might not be a place you want to visit, but I am definitely a person you want to visit!"

Red, White, and Blue

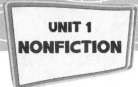

The flag of the United States of America goes by many different names. Some people call the flag the "Stars and Stripes." Some people call the flag "Old Glory." No matter what you call the flag, the American flag has a lot to tell about its country.

America started with thirteen original colonies. The colonies were part of England. The King of England ruled over these early settlements.

The thirteen colonies wanted to be independent of England. The Revolutionary War brought about their eventual independence. The thirteen stripes on the flag remind anyone who sees them that the country began with the thirteen original colonies. My, how the country has grown since 1776!

Another important part of the flag of the United States of America is the stars. There are fifty white stars positioned on a blue background. Each star has five points. The stars represent the fifty states. The flag did not begin with fifty stars. As each new state was added to the country, a star was added to the flag. If a new state was added today, the number of stripes would stay the same, but a new star would need to be added to the flag!

Each state has its own special flag. Alaska's flag has eight gold stars. Seven of the stars show the Big Dipper. The last gold star is the North Star. Tennessee's flag has stars on it, too. The stars on this flag show the three major land divisions of this state. A person can learn a lot just by studying the flags of each state!

The following pages have questions based on the texts from Unit 1. You may look at the stories to help answer any questions. Use the back of the page if you need extra space for writing your answers.

1 Which sentence best explains why Lana's grandparents have a home on wheels?

   (a) They lived in a mobile home.

   (b) "Your grandmother and I want to see all fifty states."

   (c) "Each time you visit a state, you get a magnet."

   (d) "I miss you when you are gone," Lana said.

2 Which information from the text "Red, White, and Blue" would Lana's grandparents find the most interesting?

   (a) the part that tells about the thirteen stripes on the American flag

   (b) the part that tells about the thirteen colonies becoming free from England

   (c) the part that tells how each star has five points

   (d) the part that tells the meaning behind the stars on the state flags of Alaska and Tennessee

3 Which sentence from the story helped you to answer #2?

   (a) When they came to visit, they would park their house in Lana's parents' driveway.

   (b) Lana wished they would never go away, but she knew how much they loved to travel.

   (c) "We want to learn everything we can about each state."

   (d) "We have eleven more states to visit before we can say we have seen all the states in America."

4 Explain why having a house on wheels would help Lana's grandparents be able to visit the different states.

_____

_____

5 Which adjective would best describe Lana's grandparents?

   (a) quiet   (c) mysterious

   (b) scared   (d) adventurous

6 Why are there thirteen stripes on the flag of the United States of America?

_____

_____

7 Why is Lana unable to see her grandparents as much as she would like to see them?

_____

_____

8 Write underneath each flag a fact you learned from the text "Red, White, and Blue."

_____   _____   _____

_____   _____   _____

_____   _____   _____

9 Flags have symbols. The stars on the Alaskan flag are symbols. The stripes on the American flag are symbols. The stars are also symbols.

What is a symbol? _____

_____

10 Would Lana's grandparents be happier if they did not travel so much? Give at least one reason from the story to support your answer.

_____

_____

_____

_____

Time to Write!

Part 1

Choose one of America's fifty states. Research the state you chose. Write four facts about the state.

Name of State: _____

State Facts:

1. _____

   _____

2. _____

   _____

3. _____

   _____

4. _____

   _____

Part 2

Look at the state flag for the state you chose in Part 1. Read about the symbols on the state's flag. Use the space below to draw a new flag for the state. Color the flag when you are done. Use the lines below to explain your new design.

Opening Night

Seth was nervous. It was opening night for the school play. Every year, the third-graders performed a play for the entire school and invited guests. People looked forward to seeing the play. All of the students couldn't wait to be in the third grade. The play was fun to be in and fun to watch. Seth could not believe it was finally his turn to be in the play. His two older brothers had already had their chance. Now it was his turn. He also had a big role. He was Old MacDonald, the farmer who had many animals to watch over.

The curtain rose. Seth walked out onto the stage. He looked out over the crowd and saw his parents and his brothers. They were in the front row. They waved to him, but he did not wave back. He knew he was supposed to be the farmer right now and not himself. He was glad they were waving at him, even if he couldn't wave back.

Seth stood over the microphone. He began to say his first lines. Everything was going well when he felt a small breeze on his back. He kept talking, but he reached back with one of his hands. Oh, no! He could feel a rip in the back of his shirt! During the second part of the play, he had to turn his back to the crowd. They would all see the rip in his shirt.

The lights went down, and Seth walked off the stage before the next act began. Mrs. Williams, his teacher, walked over and told him what a great job he was doing. She could tell that something was wrong, so he quickly told her about the hole in his shirt.

Mrs. Williams told him to wait right there. She left for just a moment. Then she came right back. She had a small sewing box. She pulled out three safety pins from the box. She used the pins to hold the material together. Seth could tell the hole was gone. He wouldn't have to worry about his costume. Being in the play was the best thing ever. Now he could enjoy it!

Seth barely had time to thank his teacher, and then it was time to go back on stage. Seth had known the play was going to be exciting; he hadn't known it would be exciting in more ways than one!

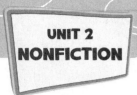

The Perfect Pin

Some inventions are found by accident. That is how the safety pin was invented back in 1849. A man named Walter Hunt wanted to improve the rifle. He needed to make a clasp out of wire that could be opened and closed. He needed the clasp to work over and over again without breaking.

Walter worked for many hours on the invention. He needed the wire clasp to open easily. The clasp would be used for rifles for the army. This meant the wire had to work well.

When Hunt was done, he had invented something new. He did not invent something to improve a rifle. Instead, the wire clasp that Hunt created would become something that all types of people would use over and over again. Walter Hunt invented the safety pin!

Even though the safety pin was invented in the 1800s, it is still used today. Years ago, people even used safety pins to hold together diapers worn by babies. People now use safety pins for many everyday reasons. The pin is a good way to hold together different pieces of materials. The safety pin is better than a straight pin because people are protected from the sharp point of the pin. The clasp closes up safe and tight. What a wonderful gadget Walter Hunt was able to make. It is especially amazing because he wasn't even trying to create the safety pin!

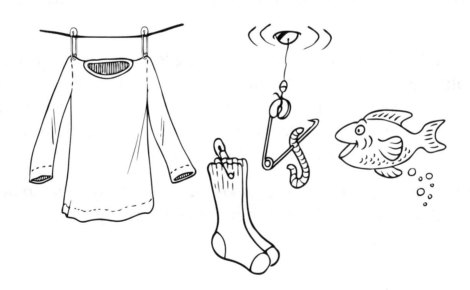

Name	Date

The following pages have questions based on the texts from Unit 2. You may look at the stories to help answer any questions. Use the back of the page if you need extra space for writing your answers.

1 Which word best describes Walter Hunt's invention of the safety pin?

(a) lucky

(b) planned

(c) unlucky

(d) silly

2 How did Seth feel once his teacher found the safety pins to fix his costume?

(a) relieved

(b) upset

(c) troubled

(d) nervous

3 Which other invention is closely related to the safety pin?

(a) buttons

(b) tape

(c) glue

(d) scissors

4 How is a safety pin like the answer you chose for #3? Write a sentence to explain how they are the same.

_____

_____

_____

5 Which sentence best shows that Seth is glad his family is at the play?

(a) Seth was nervous.

(b) He was glad they were waving at him, even if he couldn't wave back.

(c) Now he could enjoy it!

(d) Seth barely had time to thank his teacher, and then it was time to go back on stage.

6 List three events from "Opening Night" in the order in which they happened.

a. _____

_____

b. _____

_____

c. _____

_____

7 Write a sentence that helps the reader to know that even today the safety pin is still an important invention.

_____

_____

_____

_____

8 Fill in the circle of the statement from either story that is a fact, not an opinion.

(a) The play was fun to be in and fun to watch.

(b) Walter Hunt invented the safety pin!

(c) What a wonderful gadget Walter Hunt was able to make.

(d) Being in the play was the best thing ever.

9 Think about the answer you chose for #8. Explain how you know your answer is a fact.

_____

_____

_____

10 What important item is in both stories?

_____

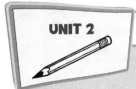
Time to Write!

What all can you do with a safety pin?

List four ways you can use a safety pin.

1. _____

2. _____

3. _____

4. _____

List four things you should NOT do with a safety pin.

1. _____

2. _____

3. _____

4. _____

Write a short speech to make everyone want to go out and buy safety pins. Convince them they need safety pins. Be sure to give good reasons why people's lives would be better if they owned the pins.

_____

_____

_____

_____

_____

_____

_____

_____

_____

Moving Day

Candy knew she should be sad, but she wasn't. Today, her family was moving to the state of New York. They would be at their new home any minute. She had lived in Kentucky since she was born. Even though she was only eleven years old, Candy had been to many places around the world because her parents loved to travel. Going to different places was not new to her. However, moving to a different place was definitely a new experience. Candy knew she would miss her old house and her old friends. She hoped the new place would feel like home soon.

Three months ago, Candy and her parents had gone to New York to look for a house. When most people think about New York, they think about the city, tall buildings, and lots of people. Candy and her family were not moving to the city. They were moving to a large farm in the northern part of the state. The best part of the move was that Candy would finally live near her grandparents. Her grandparents' farm was only a few miles from her new house. Her aunt and uncle also lived in the same town. They had a daughter the same age as Candy. She would have a cousin who would be in her same grade when she started her new school.

The car her father was driving turned into a long driveway. With her nose pressed against the car window, Candy looked at her new home. Standing on the porch were her grandparents, her aunt and uncle, and her cousin.

Her father put the car in park, and Candy quickly opened the door. She could not wait to see everyone again. Candy was certain that today was more than a moving day; it was the start of a new adventure!

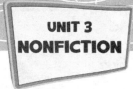

The Empire State

The state of New York is in the northeastern part of the United States of America. The state's nickname is the Empire State because of the many resources and wealth of the state. The capital city of New York is Albany. Many people think only of the "Big Apple" or New York City when they hear the words "New York." Yet this state is famous for many other reasons.

The Statue of Liberty is in New York Harbor. The famous statue is the first thing many people see when they come to America by boat. The statue was a gift from the country of France. Ellis Island is also located in New York Harbor. Ellis Island was once the first stop for people moving to America. The building is now a tourist attraction. Many people visit Ellis Island each year to see what this was like for those coming to America.

Ellis Island

Niagara Falls is also in New York. The falls are actually made of three waterfalls. Two of the falls are in New York. The other waterfall is in Canada. The falls are a beautiful part of the state. Over the years, people have done some unusual and dangerous things at Niagara Falls. People have even attempted to go over the falls in nothing except a barrel! Some survived their daredevil attempts, but others were not so lucky.

Niagara Falls

New York has much to offer people who live there. Visitors to New York are also lucky to experience all the wonders of the state. If you have never been to New York, maybe someday you will be lucky enough to go!

The following pages have questions based on the texts from Unit 3. You may look at the stories to help answer any questions. Use the back of the page if you need extra space for writing your answers.

1 Which sentence best explains why New York is called the Empire State?

   (a) The state of New York is in the northeastern part of the United States of America.

   (b) The state's nickname is the Empire State because of the many resources and wealth of the state.

   (c) The capital city of New York is Albany.

   (d) The Statue of Liberty is in New York Harbor.

2 Based on the text "The Empire State," which statement is correct?

   (a) The capital of New York is New York City.

   (b) People who immigrate to America must still go through Ellis Island.

   (c) The Statue of Liberty was a gift from England.

   (d) Part of Niagara Falls is in Canada.

3 Write the sentence or sentences you found in the text that best helped you to find the correct answer for #2.

_____

_____

_____

4 Circle the face that best shows how Candy feels about moving to New York.

5 Write a sentence from the text that best supports the answer you chose for #4.

_____

_____

_____

6 Based on the text, which word best describes how Candy feels about moving near her relatives?

(a) sad   (c) excited

(b) nervous   (d) scared

7 What is the purpose of this sentence from the story "Moving Day"?

With her nose pressed against the car window, Candy looked at her new home.

(a) It shows Candy doesn't want to miss seeing anything as she arrives at her new home.

(b) It shows that Candy wants to write on the car window.

(c) It shows that Candy wants to make a funny face for her relatives to see.

(d) It shows that Candy wants to get out of the car.

8 What is the main purpose of the text "The Empire State"?

(a) to inform

(b) to entertain

(c) to illustrate

(d) to persuade

9 What is most likely true about Candy?

(a) She hates for things to change.

(b) She likes new experiences.

(c) She is very shy.

(d) She is homesick.

10 Write the sentence or sentences from the text that helped you to answer #9.

_____

_____

_____

_____

Time to Write!

Look at the picture of the suitcase. Imagine you were moving, but you could only take five things with you (not including your clothes or family). What five things would you take? Write what you would take on the lines next to the suitcase.

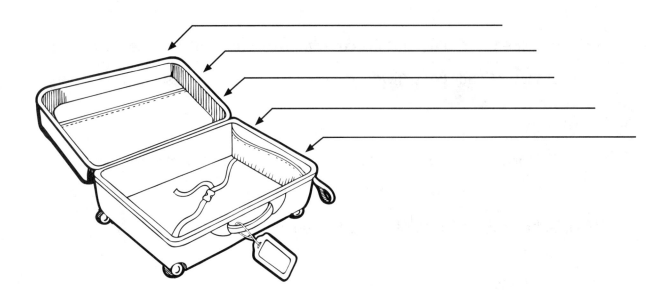

Think about the items you listed next to the suitcase. Which item is the most important to you? Use the space below to write about the item that is most important. Tell what the item is. Explain why it is so important. Tell why you would want to take it with you. Explain how you would feel if you did not have the item with you.

If I were moving, the one item I would have to take with me would be . . .

_____

_____

_____

_____

_____

_____

Something's Out There

The tent was finally up. The campfire was going. The sun had gone down. Everything was ready. Jesse couldn't believe he was finally on his first camping trip. For weeks, he'd begged his father to take him camping. Finally, his father agreed to go. Jesse's best friend, David, had been camping lots of times. He was always telling Jesse how much fun he had camping with his family.

Jesse's dad suggested they cook their hot dogs over the fire and then go for a night hike after they finished eating. His father told him there was nothing that tasted better than a hot dog cooked over an open fire. When Jesse took his first bite, he knew his father was right. It was delicious. When they finished eating, Jesse's dad helped him clean everything up.

"Make sure you put all the food inside the cooler. We don't want to leave anything out, or we might have some uninvited guests," Jesse's dad explained.

Jesse wasn't sure what he meant by "uninvited guests," but he wanted to do what his father told him to do. He put the hot dogs, buns, and other foods all back into the cooler. He made sure it was latched. Then Jesse and his father grabbed their flashlights and went for a walk.

After their walk, they were just about to enter the campsite when Jesse's father touched his arm and told him to stop. Jesse froze. His father motioned for him to be very quiet.

"Something's out there," his father whispered.

Jesse peered around his father's shoulder. He could just see their campsite. Trying to get into the cooler was a large raccoon.

"Good thing you closed it up, Jesse, or the animals would have eaten all our food, and we'd have no food for tomorrow."

Jesse grinned at his father's praise. He couldn't wait to see his best friend and tell him all about their trip and their unexpected visitor!

Camping

Many people like to go camping. There are many different ways people can enjoy this outdoor fun. Some people like to go backpack camping. They take very little with them except what they can carry on their backs. Others like to camp in tents. Some campers sleep in motor homes. They buy or rent these recreational vehicles to stay inside during their camping trips.

People can go camping during any season. A camper must make sure he has what is needed for the weather. If the trip is planned, the campers can often make reservations where they plan to stay. This will hold a spot for the campers, so they are guaranteed a place to stay. Not all camping spots have a reservation system. Some camping areas can only be rented as the campers arrive. People who backpack-camp often have to get a permit to camp. Park rangers help keep campgrounds safe for campers. Anyone who camps at a park should obey the rules and be a responsible camper.

Most people who camp know they will need special equipment. Flashlights or lanterns might be needed. Sleeping bags are also an important part of camping. These are very important for backpack or tent camping. Special sleeping bags are made to handle warm or cold temperatures. Campers also need good hiking shoes. They need clothes that will protect them from extreme temperatures. These are only some of the things a camper might need.

No matter what type of camping someone does, an important part of camping is to have fun. Getting outside with friends or family and enjoying nature is one of the best times a person can have. Everyone should try camping at least once.

UNIT 4 QUESTIONS

Name _____ **Date** _____

The following pages have questions based on the texts from Unit 4. You may look at the stories to help answer any questions. Use the back of the page if you need extra space for writing your answers.

1 What do both of the texts in Unit 4 have in common?

(a) They are both about family.

(b) They are both about camping.

(c) They are both about friends.

(d) They are both about vacations.

2 What does the word *recreational* mean as it is used in the following sentence?

They buy or rent these recreational vehicles to stay inside during their camping trips.

(a) something used for work

(b) something used to explain

(c) something used for fun

(d) something used for others

3 Why did Jesse's father want him to lock up all the food?

(a) He thought someone might steal their food.

(b) He thought Jesse might get into the food.

(c) He thought some of the other campers might take their food.

(d) He thought animals might get into their food.

4 Write the sentence from the text that helped you to answer #3.

_____

_____

_____

5 Use the story "Something's Out There," and write three events in the order they happened.

a. _____

b. _____

c. _____

6 According to "Camping," what are three types of camping many people do?

    a. _____

    b. _____

    c. _____

7 Which type of camping requires a permit?

_____

8 Using information from the text, write three things someone would need for camping.

    a. _____

    b. _____

    c. _____

9 What do the words *uninvited guests* mean as used in the following sentence:

"We don't want to leave anything out, or we might have some uninvited guests," Jesse's dad explained.

    (a) visitors you want to see

    (b) visitors you do not want to see

    (c) visitors you know

    (d) visitors from another country

10 Which sentence is an opinion?

    (a) Everyone should try camping at least once.

    (b) People can go camping during any season.

    (c) A reservation will hold a spot for the campers, so they are guaranteed a place to stay.

    (d) Park rangers help keep campgrounds safe for campers.

Time to Write!

Imagine you are on a camping trip. You are camping in a tent. You are ready to go to sleep when suddenly you hear a noise in the woods! Write about your trip and what happens next. Use the first few lines to help you get started with your story.

Story Title: _____

By: _____

The full moon was the only light shining through the trees. I was just about to get into my sleeping bag when suddenly, I heard a noise in the woods . . .

_____

_____

_____

_____

_____

_____

_____

_____

_____

_____

_____

_____

_____

The Big Report

Mrs. Sanders' third-grade class was unusually quiet. Everyone knew it was time for the reports to begin. Sam wondered who would go first. He had never given a speech before in front of the class. He hoped he wouldn't be scared to talk in front of his friends. He liked Mrs. Sanders very much, and he knew she talked in front of the class every day! She was a good teacher. She always made everyone feel proud of their work. He hoped she would be proud of him today.

Sam heard Mrs. Sanders call his name. He was not surprised that he was first. His last name was Abner. Whenever teachers went alphabetically, he always had to go first. Sam picked up his poster and moved to the front of the classroom. Mrs. Sanders attached his poster to the wall. Sam moved to the side so he could see his poster but also still look at the class. He was ready to begin.

"Daniel Boone was a famous frontiersman who was born in 1734." Sam's voice was steady and sure as he began his speech. He had loved learning about Daniel Boone. He had known very little about the man before he began his research. His favorite story was the one he was about to share with his class.

"Daniel and his family lived at Fort Boonesboro. Daniel's daughter Jemima and two of her friends left the safety of the fort. They were captured by American Indians. Jemima knew her father would come for her. She knew he would use his excellent skills as a tracker to find her. When the Indians were not looking, she left small pieces of material on the trail for her father to see. Two days after she was taken by the Indians, Daniel Boone rescued Jemima and her friends."

Sam finished his report, and everyone in the class clapped. Sam looked at Mrs. Sanders. She smiled and told him what a wonderful job he had done. She enjoyed learning so much about Daniel Boone. As Sam went to his seat, he wondered what the next school project would be. He couldn't wait to have another chance to talk in front of the class.

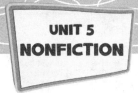
Daniel Boone

Daniel Boone was born in 1734. He was born into a family of eleven children. His father came to live in America when he was a young man. Daniel was born in America when the colonies still belonged to England.

As a boy, Daniel loved being outside. One of his chores was to help take care of the cattle. Daniel loved staying outside in the woods while he did his chores. There was no better place to be than outside with nature. His love for the outdoors would always stay with him.

During Daniel's life, the colonies were in a war known as the French and Indian War. Daniel joined the fight to keep the British colonists safe. During the war, he saw and met many different types of people. He heard people talk about a land now known as Kentucky. Kentucky had lots of animals to hunt and trap. Once the war was over, Daniel moved to this land.

Daniel Boone married a woman named Rebecca. Daniel and Rebecca had ten children. He would later live at Fort Boonesboro. It was during his time at Fort Boonesboro that his daughter Jemima and two of her friends were captured by Indians. Daniel and a few other men were able to find the girls and see to their safe return.

Daniel and his family moved to Missouri. He would live the last years of his life there. Even though Daniel Boone died in 1820, he is still remembered today. He was a great frontiersman who helped many people move west across the Appalachian Mountains.

UNIT 5 QUESTIONS

Name _____

Date _____

The following pages have questions based on the texts from Unit 5. You may look at the stories to help answer any questions. Use the back of the page if you need extra space for writing your answers.

1 What is the same about the two texts?

  (a) They are both about the Wild West.

  (b) They both share information about school.

  (c) They are both about giving a report.

  (d) They both share information about Daniel Boone.

2 When the speech is over, how does Sam feel about giving another report?

  (a) afraid

  (b) upset

  (c) nervous

  (d) excited

3 Which sentence from the text best helped you to answer #2?

  _____

  _____

  _____

  _____

4 Which would be a good alternative title for the text "Daniel Boone"?

  (a) "The Brave Frontiersman"

  (b) "The Best Father Ever"

  (c) "How to Give a Speech"

  (d) "The Big Fight"

5 List one way Sam and Daniel Boone are alike. Use the text to support your answer.

  Sam and Daniel Boone are both alike because _____

  _____

  _____.

6 Which sentence below would Sam NOT agree with?

(a) Giving a speech is not fun.

(b) Giving a speech can be a lot of fun.

(c) It is good to learn about new things.

(d) School is a great place to learn.

7 What does the word *captured* mean as it is used in the following sentence?

It was during his time at Fort Boonesboro that his daughter Jemima and two of her friends were captured by Indians.

(a) taken

(b) hidden

(c) frozen

(d) hurt

8 Which word best describes Sam's teacher, Mrs. Sanders?

(a) mean

(b) quiet

(c) caring

(d) shy

9 Which statement is an opinion?

(a) Daniel Boone was born in 1734.

(b) There was no better place to be than outside with nature.

(c) Daniel and Rebecca had ten children.

(d) Daniel and his family moved to Missouri.

10 Write a fact from the text "Daniel Boone" that is not mentioned in #9.

_____

_____

_____

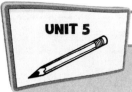
Time to Write!

With the help of your teacher, choose an important person from history who is no longer living. Use the space below to help write about the person you chose.

Name of Person: _____

Born: _____

Died: _____

List four facts:

1. _____

_____

2. _____

_____

3. _____

_____

4. _____

_____

Use the information you have gathered and write a short report. Use the space below to help you get started.

_____ is best known for _____.

       (name of person)   (most important fact)

Some other interesting information about _____

                                     (name of person)

are the following facts: _____

_____

_____

_____

The Prickly Present

Carla and her parents were shopping for plants. Spring was coming. Carla's parents liked to work outside in their yard. They wanted to buy lots of new plants and flowers to make their yard look beautiful. Carla loved the outdoors, but she had terrible allergies. She would sneeze and cough if she stayed outside too long. She loved the pretty plants her parents bought. She wished she could spend as much time outside as they did taking care of them.

Carla helped her parents unload the plants at their house. Once the truck was unloaded, Carla's father said they should go into the kitchen and make some lunch. Carla agreed. She was very hungry after spending all morning shopping.

Everyone made a sandwich and sat at the table to eat. When they were finished, Carla's father went outside and then came back into the kitchen. He was hiding something behind his back. Her parents were always surprising her. Carla wondered what her father had this time.

"Carla," her father said, "your mother and I know how much you love plants. We wanted to give you one of your own that you could take care of inside of the house."

Carla watched as her father showed her what he had been hiding. It was a cactus! It was like no plant that Carla had ever seen. It was short with small thorns all over it. On the very top of the oval surface was a lovely pink flower.

"This is a pincushion cactus," her mother explained. "You can keep it in your room because you get plenty of sunlight from your window. Remember, the plant will need very little water and very sandy soil. You must take special care of it. Your cactus needs lots of sunlight to live."

Carla couldn't wait to take care of her new plant. She wondered whether the cactus would bloom all the time. She carefully took the plant from her father and carried it up to her room. She could not wait to start taking care of her indoor plant.

The Sahara Desert

The Sahara Desert in Africa is the largest desert in the world. The word *Sahara* comes from a word that means desert. It covers so much space that it is about the size of the United States!

The Sahara is not just all flat sand. There are many different types of landscapes. There are even mountain ranges in the huge desert. In some parts of the Sahara, you can find oases. An oasis is a place in the desert where water and plants such as cacti can grow. People live in these areas. Because of the water, they can grow crops here. They can also have animals where there is water. Some of the people who live in the Sahara have herds of sheep, goats, camels, and even cattle.

Also, wild animals call the Sahara their home. Types of gazelles and antelope live on the sandy land. Snakes and lizards also live there. The animals that live in the Sahara are able to go without water for long periods of time. They get some of the water they need from the plants they eat. Most animals hunt for food during the night when the temperatures are much cooler.

The vast area that makes up the Sahara Desert is an amazing place. It is hard to imagine that the desert has so many people and animals that call the desert their home. Despite the harsh conditions, there is much beauty in the desert.

UNIT 6 QUESTIONS

Name _____ **Date** _____

The following pages have questions based on the texts from Unit 6. You may look at the stories to help answer any questions. Use the back of the page if you need extra space for writing your answers.

1 Based on the text, what is a conclusion one could come to about the Sahara Desert?

  (a) No one could ever live in the Sahara.

  (b) The land is very dry but very small.

  (c) Both people and animals live in the Sahara.

  (d) The Sahara has nothing but miles and miles of sand.

2 Which statement is true about Carla?

  (a) She does not like shopping with her parents.

  (b) She can't be outside as much as she would like to be.

  (c) She wants to be able to take care of her own outdoor plant.

  (d) Her father wants her to help him more with the work outside.

3 List three things that can be found in the Sahara Desert.

  a. _____

  b. _____

  c. _____

4 What does the word *vast* mean as it is used in the following sentence?

The vast area that makes up the Sahara Desert is an amazing place.

  (a) small

  (b) large

  (c) lonely

  (d) dry

5 Using information from the text, explain why the title of the story was "The Prickly Present."

_____

_____

_____

6 Which sentence could best be added to the end of paragraph 1 of "The Sahara Desert"?

(a) The Sahara is truly one of the most unique places in the world.

(b) The Sahara Desert is just one of many deserts in the world.

(c) A desert is a hot, dry place.

(d) Don't you wish you could go and visit the Sahara Desert?

7 Why is a cactus a plant that can easily grow in the desert?

(a) It needs a lot of water.

(b) It does not need a lot of water.

(c) It has a beautiful bloom.

(d) It likes a lot of shade.

8 Write two things Carla will need to do to take good care of her new plant.

a. _____

b. _____

9 Based on the text, what will Carla most likely do?

(a) help her father more with the outside plants

(b) take good care of the cactus

(c) ask her parents to get rid of the cactus

(d) plant the cactus outside with the other new plants

10 What would most likely be the effect of giving a cactus too much water?

_____

_____

_____

_____

Time to Write!

With your teacher's help, research a type of cactus. Then use the space below to make a brochure about the plant you have researched.

Type of Cactus:

_____

Three things I learned about this cactus:

1. _____

_____

2. _____

_____

3. _____

_____

The real name of this cactus is

_____, but if I

could name this plant, I would call it

_____ because

_____

_____

_____

_____ .

Draw and color a picture of the cactus you learned about.

Make a comparison. My cactus

reminds me of _____

_____ .

Two reasons it reminds me of this are . . .

1. _____

_____

2. _____

_____

The Blue Ribbon

It was time to hear who had won the blue ribbon. Jim could not wait to hear who had won the contest. He hoped he would hear his name. He didn't know whether he would win or not. There had been so many great pictures entered into the school's art contest. Jim was proud of the picture he had turned in to Mr. Jackson, the school's art teacher. Mr. Jackson told Jim he sent the pictures outside the school to be judged. He told Jim he did not know who would win but that Jim's picture was amazing.

Jim could not believe four weeks had passed by since the contest had been announced. The rules were for each student to make a new cartoon character. The cartoons were to be drawn in pencil and then colored with crayons or markers. The top three winners would all be given ribbons. The first-place winner would also get another prize. The new cartoon would be used throughout the school. Posters would be made with the new cartoon character on the poster. The cartoon character would be used to send positive messages throughout the school. The cartoon would even be used in a new recycling project for the school. Jim could just imagine his cartoon on all the posters. He crossed his fingers and waited for the announcements to continue.

The principal said the names of the third- and second-place winners. Jim's name was not part of the list.

"And, the first-place ribbon goes to the cartoon drawn by third-grader Jim Cannon!"

Jim could not believe it. He had won the contest! It was the first time he had ever won a blue ribbon. He was so happy and proud that his picture would be used to help around the school. He hoped the school would have another contest very soon.

Cartoons

There are many types of cartoons. Cartoons can be single pictures or series of drawings. A cartoon can be drawn to make people laugh. It can also be used to teach or show someone something important. Some cartoons also have words along with the pictures. Other cartoons have only pictures. Because most people like cartoons, they can be used in many different ways.

One type of cartoon that is different from the other types is animated cartoons. Animated cartoons have movement. They might be found on television or in movies. People of all ages enjoy watching cartoons. Many people have favorite cartoon characters they like to watch over and over.

Cartoons have been around for many years. Cartoon drawings were even found on walls in ancient Egypt! People later used cartoons to try to get people to go along with certain ideas. Benjamin Franklin drew cartoons for the early colonists. He used his cartoons to try to get people to help England during the French and Indian War. Later, the colonists would use cartoons to try to get people to fight against England. These early cartoons were not trying to be funny. They were used to help people understand what was happening in the world.

Today, cartoons are very popular. There are television stations that only show cartoons. There are comic books that are filled with popular cartoon characters. Even places like grocery stores and restaurants use cartoons to get people to buy things. Cartoons have been around for many years, and they will continue to be a part of the future.

UNIT 7
QUESTIONS

Name _____ **Date** _____

The following pages have questions based on the texts from Unit 7. You may look at the stories to help answer any questions. Use the back of the page if you need extra space for writing your answers.

1 What do the two texts have in common?

    (a) Both are about contests.

    (b) Both are about cartoons used in movies.

    (c) Both are about cartoons.

    (d) Both are about getting a blue ribbon.

2 Why is Jim excited about the art contest?

_____

_____

_____

3 Which word best shows how Jim feels when the principal announces the winner?

    (a) scared

    (b) proud

    (c) silly

    (d) curious

4 List one place a person might find an animated cartoon. Write your answer as a complete sentence.

_____

_____

_____

5 According to the text, which early American drew cartoons?

    (a) George Washington

    (b) Thomas Jefferson

    (c) Abraham Lincoln

    (d) Benjamin Franklin

6 List in order three things that happen in the story "The Blue Ribbon."

a. _____

_____

b. _____

_____

c. _____

_____

7 What will Jim most likely do the next time there is an art contest?

ⓐ He will not enter the contest.

ⓑ He will enter the contest.

ⓒ He will not care about the contest.

ⓓ He will tell his friend to enter the contest.

8 Which sentence from the story best helped you to answer #7?

_____

_____

_____

_____

9 What does the word *popular* mean as it is used in the following sentence?

Today, cartoons are very popular.

ⓐ liked   ⓒ forgotten

ⓑ disliked   ⓓ remembered

10 Using information from the text, write two places you might see a cartoon.

a. _____

b. _____

 **UNIT 7**

Name	Date

Time to Write!

Use the cartoon strip below to create your own cartoon. Use these hints to help get you started:

1. Create two cartoon characters. Draw them in the boxes below.

2. The two cartoon characters should be talking to each other. Write their words inside speech bubbles.

3. The two cartoon characters should be talking about something that happens at school.

4. Use only the space given.

5. Color the cartoon when you are finished.

Missy had always dreamed of flying. Whenever she and her family went on vacation, they always drove. Missy's mother was scared of flying. Even if they went very far on their trips, they still went in a car. Missy knew she would never get to fly anywhere on vacation. In fact, she wondered if she would ever get to fly at all.

One day, Missy's father came to school to pick her up. She was surprised to hear her name called out. She was even more surprised by the huge grin that was on her father's face when she opened the car door and slid into her seat.

"How was your day, Missy?" her father asked.

"Good," Missy answered quickly. "But, Dad, why are you here? You don't usually pick me up from school."

Her dad's grin grew even wider. "I have a surprise for you. Today, I am going to take you flying!"

Missy could not believe it. Her father quickly explained that he was taking her to fly in a helicopter. He had bought tickets for them to fly over the city. The ride in the helicopter would last for one hour. He had been waiting for the weather to be perfect before telling her about the trip.

Her father also explained that her mother would meet them there to take lots of pictures of the big day. Her father would be the person flying with Missy in the helicopter.

Missy could not believe she was going to fly. She had thought she would never get the chance. She had never dreamed of going up in a helicopter. What a great idea, and what a great way to fly for the first time!

Finally, she would get her chance to fly high in the sky!

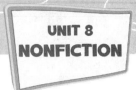
Whirlybird

The sound of a helicopter flying overhead causes nearly everyone to look up. The whirl of the large rotors on top makes a powerful noise. The nicknames of "whirlybird" and "chopper" can be easily understood once someone sees the powerful machine flying through the air.

The helicopter flies in a different way than an airplane. The large mechanical bird can fly straight up or straight down. It can also move forward, backward, and even sideways. A helicopter can also stay in one place or hover. A helicopter can land or take off in a very small space. Those are things an airplane cannot do.

Today, you might see a helicopter flying and looking at traffic. The pilot is able to get a close look at what is happening on the roads. The pilot can report what he or she sees so that others can know which roads are bad. Helicopters can also be used for medical emergencies. Someone who needs help can be taken to a hospital very quickly in a helicopter. The helicopter can land on a special site at the hospital that is just for helicopters.

The military also uses helicopters for many of their missions. If you live near a military base, you may have helicopters fly near your house. Military helicopters are used for many special things. They can carry people or supplies. Some might even carry weapons.

A helicopter can be used in many different ways. One thing is certain, though. This bird in the sky is an amazing way to fly.

The following pages have questions based on the texts from Unit 8. You may look at the stories to help answer any questions. Use the back of the page if you need extra space for writing your answers.

1 Why is Missy's father smiling when he picks her up from school?

    (a) He is happy to see her.

    (b) He knows she will be happy to be a passenger.

    (c) He knows it is her birthday.

    (d) He has a surprise for her.

2 Why is Missy's mother not going on the ride with Missy and her father?

    (a) She could not get a ticket.

    (b) She had to work.

    (c) She is sick.

    (d) She does not like to fly.

3 What do both texts have in common?

    (a) They both have something to do with flying.

    (b) They both are about special surprises.

    (c) They both are about making friends.

    (d) They both have something to do with keeping secrets.

4 Using the text, list two ways a helicopter is different from an airplane.

    a. _____

    _____

    b. _____

    _____

5 Why had Missy's father waited to tell her about the helicopter ride?

_____

_____

_____

6 How does Missy feel about going up in a helicopter?

(a) shocked

(b) excited

(c) angry

(d) upset

7 Which sentence from the story helped you to answer #6?

_____

_____

_____

8 In the text "Whirlybird," which paragraph best explains the different ways a helicopter can be flown?

(a) paragraph 1

(b) paragraph 2

(c) paragraph 3

(d) paragraph 4

9 If Missy has the chance to fly in an airplane, how would she most likely react?

(a) She would not go.

(b) She would go only if her mother would go.

(c) She would not fly again unless she could fly in a helicopter.

(d) She would want to go.

10 Which is an opinion about helicopters?

(a) They are the best way to fly.

(b) They can land in small spaces.

(c) They can be used to move supplies.

(d) They are flown by the military.

 **Name** **Date**

Time to Write!

There are many things that can fly in the sky. Imagine you are outside, and suddenly you see a flying saucer soar across the night sky. What would you do? Where do you think the flying saucer is from? What will happen after you see the flying saucer?

Use the space below to write a story about seeing the flying saucer flying through the sky and then landing on planet Earth.

_____

_____

_____

_____

_____

_____

_____

_____

_____

_____

_____

_____

First-Day Jitters

"You're going to love school," Andy told his sister Sarah.

Sarah did not look like she believed her older brother.

Andy wasn't sure what to do. Sarah was supposed to start kindergarten tomorrow. She was very scared. Their mother had asked Andy to talk to Sarah. Their mother thought if Andy told Sarah school was great, then maybe she wouldn't be so nervous. Andy had been trying to talk to Sarah for the last fifteen minutes, but she just didn't want to listen.

"I don't want to go," Sarah said to Andy. "Why can't I just stay home?"

Andy sighed. He had already answered this question three times. He wondered if he had been this scared when he started school. Looking at his little sister, he suddenly had an idea.

"Wait right here, Sarah. I'm going to get something for you." It didn't take long for Andy to find what he was looking for. He had a chart with squares and a pack of stickers.

"I was really scared to go to the dentist when I was your age. Mom put a chart on the refrigerator for me. Each day we counted down to going to the dentist. Each day that I was brave about going, she gave me a sticker. On the day of the visit, I only had one sticker left to earn. When I got my last sticker, Mom took me to see a movie. The dentist ended up being just fine, and the movie was great!"

"But I'm not going to the dentist," Sarah said.

Andy agreed, "Yes, but you are nervous about going to school just like I was about the dentist. School starts tomorrow. Each day you come home having a great day, I'll give you a sticker. Then when you fill up the chart, you and I can plan a special day together."

Finally, Andy saw Sarah smile. He knew she would have the chart filled up in no time. He couldn't wait to plan their special day.

School

The first schools in America were started in the 1600s. The early colonists set up schools to teach reading, writing, and religion. In many parts of the United States, children did not have to go to school like they do today. Schools of long ago also looked much different than schools do today. The buildings were usually log cabins or small wooden buildings. Most were only one room. They would have a stove for heat and a few windows. Children of all different ages would go to school in the one-room school. There would be only one teacher. The teacher would teach all the subjects to all the children.

After the colonies became a country, the rules for school slowly began to change. Children could no longer stay home and work or work at factories during the day. They had to go to school. This was a good change for all children. Everyone would have a chance to learn. Children would not have to go to work in factories. Children would not have to stay at home and work on farms all day long. They would have a chance to get an education.

Today, there are many different types of schools. Some students go to public schools. Some children go to private schools. Other students have tutors or are homeschooled. Even though there are many different choices, there is one thing that is the same about all of them. All children have the chance to get an education and to learn. This is the most important thing of all about school.

UNIT 9 QUESTIONS

Name   **Date**

The following pages have questions based on the texts from Unit 9. You may look at the stories to help answer any questions. Use the back of the page if you need extra space for writing your answers.

1 Which sentence would be a good summary for the text "School"?

    (a) Schools are very different today than they were years ago.

    (b) Schools have changed very little over the years.

    (c) All children must go to school.

    (d) It is important for children to go to school.

2 In the title "First-Day Jitters," what does the word *jitters* most likely mean?

    (a) being excited to try something new

    (b) being nervous to try something new

    (c) being happy to try something new

    (d) being sad to try something new

3 Write the sentence or sentences from the text that helped you to answer #2.

_____

_____

_____

4 Which word best describes Andy's relationship with his sister?

    (a) angry

    (b) caring

    (c) relaxed

    (d) friendly

5 In the text "School," which part of the story best tells what school buildings once looked like?

    (a) the title

    (b) paragraph 1

    (c) paragraph 2

    (d) paragraph 3

6 Use the text "School" to write one reason why going to school is good for all children.

_____

_____

_____

_____

7 What does Andy compare Sarah's first day of school to?

(a) the first time he had to go to school

(b) the first time he was in a play

(c) the first time he met someone new

(d) the first time he had to go to the dentist

8 Explain what Andy wants to do to help Sarah.

_____

_____

_____

9 Why does Andy think that will work for Sarah?

_____

_____

_____

10 What do the texts have in common?

(a) Both are about being afraid to try something new.

(b) Both are about school.

(c) Both are about brothers and sisters.

(d) Both are about children having to work in factories.

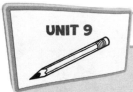

Time to Write!

Imagine you were principal of a school. What would you do if you were in charge of the school? Write in complete sentences, and fill in each section.

Part 1

Write five rules you would have at your school.

1. _____

2. _____

3. _____

4. _____

5. _____

Circle one of the rules and explain why this rule is important to the school.

_____

_____

Part 2

What would a day be like if you were principal? Write a short story telling about your new job. Use the back of the page if you need more space.

_____

_____

_____

_____

_____

_____

_____

_____

The Discovery

The sun was high in the sky as Cal and Jeff began to explore. The two boys had been best friends since first grade. They lived in the same neighborhood. They spent their afternoons together doing things like riding bikes and playing video games. Today was different. They were playing a new game.

During school they had learned about Columbus. Columbus had been a brave explorer. He wanted to find a way to reach India. Instead, Columbus and his men found a new land. Cal and Jeff did not think they would find a new land, but they wanted to explore the woods behind Jeff's house. They hoped they would find something new and exciting just like Columbus and his men had.

"What do you think we'll discover?" Cal asked Jeff.

"I don't know," Jeff answered, "but a good explorer should learn to enjoy the journey."

Cal agreed. "It is fun being out here in the woods."

Jeff and Cal saw many different animals as they explored the woods. There were deer and squirrels and even a rabbit. Jeff showed Cal all of the small bugs he discovered underneath some leaves. He had brought a magnifying glass with him. They watched as a line of ants made their way to a nearby anthill. They did not bother the ants.

The two boys were ready to end their day of exploring when Cal stumbled over a pile of rocks. Jeff leaned down with his magnifying glass to take a closer look.

"Cal! We've found something!" Jeff exclaimed.

The two boys looked closely at the rock Jeff was holding. There in the rock was the imprint of a leaf. They had found a fossil.

"We are great explorers, Jeff," Cal said. "We've found our first fossil."

Finding the Past

Years ago, there were different plants and animals on Earth. No one knows for sure why some living things disappeared. Even though many things from the past are gone, there are ways people can study the past. Fossils are one way people can study what life was like long ago.

Scientists can study the past by studying Earth. Earth has many hidden treasures. These hidden treasures are known as fossils. The bones of creatures that lived long ago can sometimes be found buried under layers of dirt, rock, or sand. Some things from the past have even been found buried under ice!

Fossils can give us a lot of information. Well-preserved fossils can show almost exactly what an animal or plant once looked like. The bones of some animals remain because they turned to stone. Animals that have died usually decompose. This means the bones slowly disappear. Animals that have been turned into fossils do not decompose. Some fossils were made as hard mud pressed down on the  bones of an animal. Over years, the bones turned into rock. The remains of the animal were trapped in the rock and saved.

Plants can also be found as fossils. Plant fossils can happen in different ways. Most people have seen fossils of plants when imprints of leaves are found on rocks. Tree sap is another way plants and even small animals or insects become fossils. The sticky sap hardens around the once living thing. The tree sap hardens, and a fossil is made.

Many prehistoric trees and plants have yet to be discovered. Maybe someday you will find a fossil of your own!

Name	Date

The following pages have questions based on the texts from Unit 10. You may look at the stories to help answer any questions. Use the back of the page if you need extra space for writing your answers.

1 Which sentence best explains how Jeff feels about being an explorer?

(a) The two boys had been best friends since first grade.

(b) Columbus had been a brave explorer.

(c) "I don't know," Jeff answered, "but a good explorer should learn to enjoy the journey."

(d) "We are great explorers, Jeff," Cal said.

2 Which would be a good alternative title for the text "The Discovery"?

(a) "Becoming an Explorer"

(b) "Fossils and Dinosaurs"

(c) "Friends and Fun"

(d) "Scared Silly"

3 Explain why the title you chose for #2 would be a good alternative title for the text. Write your answer in complete sentences.

_____

_____

_____

4 Which is a true statement about the text "Finding the Past"?

(a) Plants can also be found as fossils.

(b) Plants can never be found as fossils.

(c) There is no way to know about plants that lived years ago.

(d) Scientists are only interested in studying plants that are living today.

5 In the text "Finding the Past," what do the words *hidden treasures* mean as used in paragraph 2?

_____

_____

_____

6 In paragraph 2 of "The Discovery," why does the author write about Columbus?

    (a) because Columbus is famous

    (b) because the boys have to write a report for school about Columbus

    (c) because the boys live in a town named after Columbus

    (d) because Columbus is a famous explorer

7 What does *well-preserved* mean as it is used in this sentence?

Well-preserved fossils can show almost exactly what an animal or plant once looked like.

    (a) something that still looks good

    (b) something that does not look good

    (c) something that is invisible

    (d) something that is hidden

8 Give one reason from the texts why fossils are important to people today.

_____

_____

9 Write the sentence or sentences from the text that helped you to answer #8.

_____

_____

_____

10 Draw a circle around the picture that best shows where a fossil might be found.

Time to Write!

Most people know Christopher Columbus was a famous explorer. But did you know Columbus has his own holiday? With the help of your teacher, use the Internet to find out at least five facts about Columbus Day.

Write the facts in the space below.

1. _____

2. _____

3. _____

4. _____

5. _____

Next, compare and contrast your favorite holiday to Columbus Day. Use the Venn diagram below to help. Be sure to include the following:

- two ways the holidays are the same
- two ways each holiday is different

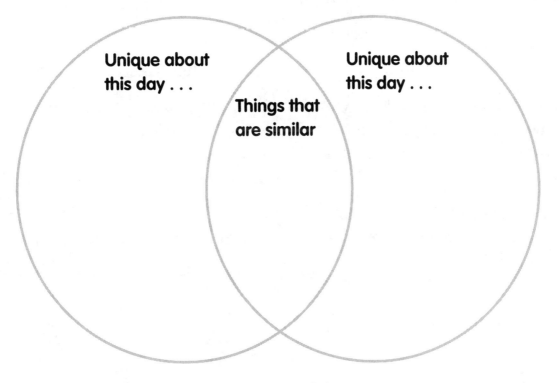

Unique about this day . . .

Things that are similar

Unique about this day . . .

Columbus Day   **Holiday:** _____

Looking for Bigfoot

Randy tried to stay awake. He was getting so sleepy, but he did not want to fall asleep. His family had been driving across the country for two days. They were headed on vacation. They were going to California for spring break.

Just last week, Randy and his mother had looked at a map. His mother showed him on the map exactly where they would be driving. He knew she would have the GPS to guide her on the trip, but he liked looking at the map. He liked being able to see all the names of the cities and towns they would be passing along the way. He also planned to use the map for something else. He wanted to know when they reached the area where the last Bigfoot sighting had been.

Randy was fascinated by all the stories of Bigfoot. Bigfoot was supposed to be a large, ape-looking creature. He was also described as much larger than any man. Randy had read that some people claimed to have seen Bigfoot near California. Randy wished he could see Bigfoot. He did not want to miss a chance to see the creature he had read so much about.

"What are you doing?" Randy's mom asked him.

Randy was staring out the car window.

"I'm trying to see Bigfoot," he said.

"What do you plan to do if you see him?" his mother asked.

Randy stopped looking out the window. He had not thought that far ahead. The drawings he had seen of Bigfoot made the creature look big and scary. All of a sudden, the idea of seeing the giant monster didn't sound very fun. What would he do if he saw Bigfoot? He would never be able to go to sleep again!

"Maybe I will just take a nap instead," Randy told his mother. Randy settled down to take a nice, long nap. He hoped he could dream about anything except Bigfoot!

Legendary Creatures

People all over the world are fascinated by legends. Some of the most popular legends are the stories about mythical creatures. Many people have claimed to see such monsters as Bigfoot, the Abominable Snowman, and the Loch Ness Monster. Some people think they have seen monsters in lakes. Others spot unusual creatures in heavily wooded areas. Some people even claim to see monsters roaming along snowy mountains. Sightings of mythical creatures seem to happen all over the world.

Loch Ness Monster

What is a legend? A legend is a story that some people believe is true even if there is no real evidence to prove the story is real. These types of stories can usually be traced back to the past when people told stories to pass along information.

Years ago, many people could not read or write. Paper was also expensive and hard to get. People shared many of their stories. People sometimes changed the facts each time they told a story. Over the years, people began to retell the stories until the story was very different than the first time someone told it. The stories were told so often that people began to believe they were true. Many of the stories had some truth but changed as they were told over and over again.

So do unusual creatures exist, or are they just stories that have been passed down from one person to another? No one knows for sure whether the creatures really exist or ever did exist. But the stories *do* exist, and they will continue to fascinate people for many years.

UNIT 11 QUESTIONS

Name _____ **Date** _____

The following pages have questions based on the texts from Unit 11. You may look at the stories to help answer any questions. Use the back of the page if you need extra space for writing your answers.

1 What lesson is learned in the story "Looking for Bigfoot"?

    (a) Be careful what you wish for.

    (b) Things aren't always what they seem.

    (c) Slow and steady wins the race.

    (d) Even the smallest creatures are important.

2 After Randy takes his nap, will he keep looking for Bigfoot? Use information from the text to explain your answer.

_____

_____

_____

3 According to the text "Legendary Creatures," what is a legend?

_____

_____

_____

4 By the end of the story, which word best describes Randy's feelings about finding Bigfoot?

    (a) curious

    (b) fascinated

    (c) interested

    (d) afraid

5 Which creature is mentioned in both texts?

    (a) the Loch Ness Monster

    (b) Bigfoot

    (c) the Abominable Snowman

    (d) an alien

6 List two reasons why Randy liked looking at a map of their trip.

a. _____

_____

b. _____

_____

7 How were most legends shared with other people?

(a) They were written as short stories.

(b) They were told out loud as stories.

(c) They were shared on the Internet.

(d) They were sent through texts to other people.

8 Why do parts of stories that are told out loud sometimes change? Fill in the circles of all the answers that could be true.

(a) People accidentally change the stories when they tell them out loud.

(b) People forget some of the details when they are telling the stories out loud.

(c) People change some of the facts of the stories to make them more interesting.

(d) People never change any parts of the stories when they are telling them out loud.

9 Write two details from the text that describe Bigfoot.

a. _____

_____

b. _____

_____

10 Which would be the best sentence to add to paragraph 2 of "Legendary Creatures"?

(a) Legends continue to exist because people still talk about them.

(b) Many legends have been made into movies.

(c) Legends are always written down.

(d) Legends are always true.

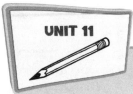

Time to Write!

Part 1

Think about where you live. For example, do you live in a city or in the country?
Do you live near the woods? Do you live near a lake? Do you have neighbors?
Write two to four sentences describing the area where you live.

_____

_____

_____

_____

_____

Part 2

Create your own legendary creature that would live near you. What is the name
of the creature? What would the creature look like? Why does it live in your
area? Where have people seen it? Does it have any enemies? How do people
feel about the creature? Write about your creature on the lines below.

_____

_____

_____

_____

_____

_____

_____

Something Extra: On the back of the page, draw and color a picture of your
new creature.

The Perfect Bow

The noise of the sewing machine filled the small bedroom. Tammy was visiting her grandmother. Her grandmother loved to sew. She had made a small bedroom into her sewing room. There were stacks of materials and more thread and buttons than Tammy had ever seen. Her grandmother had promised to teach Tammy to sew. She could not wait to learn to make some of her own clothes.

Tammy looked down at her own shirt and shorts. She was wearing one of her favorite outfits. Her grandmother had made it for her last year. She had let Tammy choose the material for the outfit. Tammy had picked a pattern with purple polka dots because purple was her favorite color. She knew she didn't want all of her clothes to be the same color, but she hoped she could make at least one more purple outfit.

"What are we going to sew?" Tammy asked her grandmother when she had stopped the machine.

Her grandmother motioned for Tammy to come stand beside her.

"Look at all of the different ribbon I bought," her grandmother said. "I thought we could sew you a beautiful new hair bow to wear.

"You can make things besides clothes?" Tammy asked.

Her grandmother laughed. "Of course. Would you like to make a bow for your hair?"

Tammy nodded yes. Her grandmother looked at all the ribbon and then looked at Tammy. "Which color do you want?"

"Purple," Tammy answered quickly, "but I don't see any purple ribbon, so I will choose a different color."

Her grandmother laughed and then reached down and picked up a sack. She opened the bag so Tammy could see. Inside were many different purple ribbons.

"I was just teasing you," her grandmother said with a smile. "I knew all along that you would want purple!"

Sewing

Sewing has been around for thousands of years. Years ago, sewing was not done by machines. Anyone wishing to sew had to sew by hand. Needles were much different than they are today. The earliest needles were made from the bones of animals. They were used to sew together furs. Some early needles were also made from the horns of animals. The earliest needles did not have eyes. The eye of a needle is the small opening where the thread passes through.

The earliest thread was also different than thread today. Thread was made from plant fibers or from animals. Catgut was used to make thread. Catgut is part of the inside intestines of some animals such as sheep or goats. Early thread was also made into different colors. People would use different berries to dye the thread and change the colors.

People began trying to invent sewing machines as early as the 1700s. These early machines were not successful. In 1834, Walter Hunt made a sewing machine. Hunt began to worry that if his machine was successful, it would put many people who sewed by hand out of work. Later, an inventor named Elias Howe would use Hunt's ideas to create his own sewing machine. It wasn't until the late 1800s that sewing machines began to be made that could be used by others.

The invention of the sewing machine is mainly given to two men. Elias Howe and Isaac Singer. Both men helped make sewing machines that could be used in factories. Sewing machines would also become used in people's homes. Earlier sewing machines relied on people hand-cranking the machines. Later inventions would add a foot pedal, so the machines would work much easier.

Today, people still do a lot of sewing in their homes. People use sewing machines to make clothes and many other items. People can even make their own curtains and pillows. Some sewing is still done by hand. However, the invention of the sewing machine made a huge difference in the lives of many people.

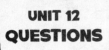

UNIT 12 QUESTIONS

Name   **Date**

The following pages have questions based on the texts from Unit 12. You may look at the stories to help answer any questions. Use the back of the page if you need extra space for writing your answers.

1 From both texts, the reader can tell that . . .

     a sewing is important to many people.

     b most people don't know about the history of sewing.

     c all girls like hair bows.

     d needles are made from the bones of animals.

2 Based on the text, people long ago most likely sewed . . .

     a by machine.

     b in factories.

     c by hand.

     d at school.

3 Which word best describes Tammy's grandmother?

     a silly

     b mean

     c caring

     d funny

4 "Catgut" could best be described as . . .

     a part of a cat.

     b plant fibers.

     c animal intestines.

     d fish scales.

5 Write the sentence from the text that helped you to answer #4.

_____

_____

_____

6 What do both stories have in common?

(a) clothes

(b) grandparents

(c) sewing

(d) inventions

7 List in order three things that happen in the story "The Perfect Bow."

a. _____

_____

b. _____

_____

c. _____

_____

8 List one detail from the text that shows Tammy's grandmother is thoughtful.

_____

_____

9 Which statement is a fact?

(a) People have been sewing for thousands of years.

(b) People have always used sewing machines to sew.

(c) Everyone was happy when the sewing machine was invented.

(d) Everyone should learn to sew.

10 Write the sentence from the text that helped you to answer #9.

_____

_____

_____

Time to Write!

Imagine you have been asked to create and sew a new costume for a superhero. Use the space below to help design the new costume.

1. Which superhero has asked you to make the costume?

   _____

2. What colors will you use to make the costume?

   _____

   _____

3. What special features will you add to the costume?

   _____

   _____

   _____

4. Describe what the costume will look like when you have finished making it.

   _____

   _____

   _____

Write a story with your superhero in it. Be sure to describe the superhero's costume in your story. Draw the costume on the back of the page.

_____

_____

_____

_____

_____

Running for the Win

Field Day was one of Jeff's favorite days at school. The day had been so much fun. All of the students in third and fourth grade had gone outside to play games. Some of the games were just for fun. Some of the games were played to win ribbons. Jeff's older brother Jackson had won a ribbon two years ago. Jeff wanted to win a blue ribbon, too. A blue ribbon would mean he had won first place. Jeff didn't just want any blue ribbon. He wanted to win first place in the last event of the day. The last event was always a race. Jeff wanted to prove he was the fastest student in his class.

Mrs. Miller blew the whistle she wore around her neck. All of the students gathered around her. Everyone was waiting to hear what she was about to say.

"We are ready to have our last event," Mrs. Miller said. "I have fifteen students signed up for the race. I will read the list of names. Then I need everyone whose name is called to go line up for the race."

Jeff heard Mrs. Miller say his name, and then he began to line up for the race. It wasn't long until all of the other participants were lined up on the starting line.

Mrs. Miller blew her whistle a second time. Everyone became very quiet. Then she said the magic words Jeff had been waiting to hear. "On your mark, get set, go!"

Jeff began to move the minute she said "go." He raced as fast as he could. He felt the breeze on his face. At first, he could see the other students racing beside him. It didn't take long before he could no longer see the others. He was in the lead. He was winning. Jeff raced across the finish line. Everyone cheered. He had really done it. He had won first place!

Mrs. Miller placed the blue ribbon in his hand and told him how proud she was of him.

Jeff was proud, too. He had done what he set out to do. He really did feel like a winner!

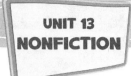

An Olympic Hero

Jesse Owens was the tenth child of Henry and Emma Owens. Jesse was born in 1913. Jesse's family did not have much money. His father was a sharecropper. This meant his family did not own the land his family lived on. Instead, they lived on someone else's land. Jesse's family grew a small cotton crop on the land where they lived. Each year, his father would sell the crop and give a portion of the money he made to the person who owned the land where he lived. The rest of the money would be used to buy food and other things the family might need. Because there was very little money, Jesse's parents could not save any to try to help their children.

When Jesse was born, he was not healthy. He had trouble with his lungs. There was no money to get a doctor to help Jesse. Mr. Owens wanted to do more for his family. He decided the family needed to move away from the country to a bigger city. In 1922, he moved his family to Cleveland, Ohio.

Jesse went to school in Ohio. When he was fourteen, the coach of the school's track team asked Jesse to join the team. Jesse still had trouble with his lungs. Running and practicing each day helped Jesse's lungs get stronger. Each day, he grew stronger and stronger. By the time he was in high school, he was an important member of the track team. He was also good at broad jumps. He began to break many records when he would compete. In fact, Jesse became so good at his sport that, in 1936, he was invited to join the Olympic track and field team for the United States.

That year, the Olympic Games were held in Germany. Adolf Hitler was the German leader. Hitler believed that no other group of people were as good as the Germans. He did not want Jesse to win any medals because Jesse was African-American. But that did not stop Jesse. Jesse Owens was a true superstar in the Olympic Games. He won many gold medals for the United States. He became a true hero for all Americans, and he is still a hero today.

The following pages have questions based on the texts from Unit 13. You may look at the stories to help answer any questions. Use the back of the page if you need extra space for writing your answers.

1 List three things that happened chronologically in Jesse Owens' life.

a. _____

_____

b. _____

_____

c. _____

_____

2 What do the two texts have in common?

(a) Both are about the Olympic Games.

(b) Both are about people who want to win.

(c) Both are about the importance of family.

(d) The two stories have nothing in common.

3 Why is Jesse Owens an Olympic hero? Use information from the text to explain your answer.

_____

4 What does the word *sharecropper* mean as it is used in the following sentence?

His father was a sharecropper.

(a) someone who sells the crop he raises to other farmers

(b) someone who lives on and farms someone else's land

(c) someone who lets another person raise a crop on his land

(d) someone who helps another person raise a crop

5 Why is Jeff most excited about Field Day?

(a) He likes playing outside.

(b) He likes being with his friends.

(c) He wants to win a blue ribbon.

(d) He wants to make his teacher proud.

6 What would winning a blue ribbon mean?

    (a) It would mean Jeff finished the race.

    (b) It would mean Jeff won the race.

    (c) It would mean Jeff won second place in the race.

    (d) It would mean Jeff could run the race more than once.

7 What do Jeff and Jesse have in common?

    (a) They both like to run.

    (b) They both participated in the Olympic Games.

    (c) They both had large families.

    (d) They both had problems with their lungs.

8 Using information from the text, why did Mr. Owens most likely move his family to the city?

_____

_____

_____

9 In the story "Running for the Win," what does the word *lead* mean as it is used in the following sentence?

He was in the lead.

    (a) to be in first place

    (b) to be in command

    (c) to be an example

    (d) to be in charge

10 Write the sentence(s) from the story that helped you to answer #9.

_____

_____

_____

Time to Write!

The five rings are used as the Olympic symbol. Each ring represents the main continents that are part of the Olympic Games. The rings are also colored blue, yellow, black, green, and red. These colors are found in the flags of the countries that are part of the Olympic Games.

Imagine you have been asked to create a new symbol for the next Games. Use the space below to draw and color your new symbol. Write at least five sentences explaining what your new symbol means.

_____

_____

_____

_____

_____

_____

Misty was having so much fun! The new toy her father had bought her was called a hula hoop. Misty had never seen one. She'd heard about the toy from several of her friends. Her father told her he and his sisters had all had hula hoops when they were younger. He had seen this one in the store and thought Misty would love it.

At first, Misty hadn't known what to do with the new toy. The hula hoop was a large circle made from plastic. Her father had to show her what to do. Once she understood how it worked, Misty stepped into the circle and began to spin the hula hoop around her waist. To keep the hoop moving, she had to move her hips much as a hula dancer would. It didn't take her long to become an expert. After only a few days, she could use the hula hoop longer than anyone else in her family.

Misty's school was having a talent show. Misty had signed up to be in the show. She had not known then what she would do for her talent. The hula hoop gave her an idea.

She asked her father if he would buy her two more hula hoops. He said he would. Then Misty decided which music she wanted to use for the talent show. It did not take long for her to have everything she would need for the show.

On the night of the talent show, Misty was only a little nervous. She had been practicing her talent for several days. When it was her turn to go on stage, Misty walked on with three hula hoops. The music began to play, and Misty began to show off her skills with each hoop. Misty could now use three of the hoops all at once. She could even twirl the plastic circles around her arms and legs.

The crowd loved Misty's talent. Everyone cheered and clapped when Misty's act was over. Misty found her father in the crowd and gave him a big hug. She knew her special night was all thanks to him and the wonderful gift he had given her.

The Hoop

Have you ever wondered where the hula hoop came from? Believe it or not, the circular toy has been around for a long time. As early as Ancient Greece, people were using hoops to help keep themselves tone and fit. Back then, it was not called a hula hoop.

As people began to explore other lands, they saw many amazing things. Early British explorers landed in the Hawaiian Islands. That's when they first saw the women dancing. Their dance was called the hula. The sailors noticed the motions of the hula dancers were similar to what was called hooping back home. After this, the toy became quickly known after the hula dance!

Over the years, the look of the hoop began to change. The first hoops, of course, were not made out of plastic. Instead, they were made from various materials. Some were made from bamboo, vines, and even wood. It was much later that the hoops became the plastic-made shapes we are all familiar with now.

A toy company helped make the hoop a well-known toy. The toy company claimed the brand name, making the hoop officially a "Hula Hoop." Today, people still use the hoops for both fun and exercise.

UNIT 14 QUESTIONS

Name

Date

The following pages have questions based on the texts from Unit 14. You may look at the stories to help answer any questions. Use the back of the page if you need extra space for writing your answers.

1 What does the word *circular* mean as it is used in the following sentence?

Believe it or not, the circular toy has been around for a long time.

 (a) square

 (b) cylinder

 (c) circle

 (d) oval

2 What does Misty decide to do with her new toy?

 (a) She shares it with her sister.

 (b) She donates it to a charity.

 (c) She takes it to her dance class.

 (d) She uses it as her talent.

3 List three things that happen in order in the story "Fun and Games."

a. _____

_____

b. _____

_____

c. _____

_____

4 Which happened *before* the hoops were made of plastic?

 (a) A toy company gave the toy hoop its name.

 (b) Ancient Greeks used the hoops to help keep themselves fit.

 (c) The toy hoop was sold in stores.

 (d) People bought the toy hoops as gifts.

5 What do both texts have in common?

_____

_____

6 Write two adjectives that describe the toy hoop.

a. _____

b. _____

7 Write two details that show how Misty used the hoops in the talent show.

a. _____

b. _____

8 Which sentence best describes the main idea of the story "Fun and Games"?

(a) Never lose hope.

(b) Be who you are, not who others want you to be.

(c) Be kind to your neighbors.

(d) A good idea can be found in many places.

9 If Misty were given another gift by her father, what would she most likely do?

(a) not open the gift

(b) be excited about the gift

(c) give the gift to someone else

(d) ask her father for a different gift

10 Which picture would be a good illustration to go with the text "The Hoop"?

(a)   (b)   (c)   (d)

Time to Write!

Part 1

Look at the list of toys below. With the help of your teacher, choose a toy to research. Write what you have learned in the space below.

bicycle	jump rope	roller skates	yo-yo
jacks	marbles	slingshot	other: _____

Name of the toy I am researching: _____

Part 2

Draw and color a picture of the toy you have chosen.

Part 3

As you research the toy you have chosen, write down the facts you learn in the space provided.

1. _____

_____

2. _____

_____

3. _____

_____

4. _____

_____

5. _____

_____

6. _____

_____

Farming Fun

"What are we going to get out of our garden today?" Joy asked her mother.

Joy's mother stopped in front of a row of plants. "These are peanut plants," she told Joy. "Most of the other plants have stopped giving us any food. Peanuts are harvested in the fall. We will get lots of peanuts from just one plant."

Joy stared at the green leaves. She had thought the plants were clovers. She had not known they were actual plants that would give food. She could not wait to see how many peanuts there would be.

Joy took a small spade from her mother. She had on her gardening gloves to help keep her hands clean. She got on her knees and pulled back the top of the plant. She dug the spade into the dirt. Then she pulled gently on the top of the plant. She dug some more and pulled some more. Then, to her surprise, the plant came loose from the soil.

"Look at all the peanuts," Joy's mother said.

There were shells all underneath the plant. Joy knew when she opened the shells they would be filled with the tasty peanuts. She was amazed at how many peanuts were underneath just one plant.

"What do you think we should do with all these peanuts?" her mother asked. She pointed to the two rows of peanut plants as she asked Joy the question.

Joy knew exactly what she wanted to do with their new harvest. "Eat them!"

Her mother nodded her head and agreed that eating them was the best idea of all.

The Amazing Peanut

George Washington Carver was born into slavery. As he grew up, George had a passion for education. He wanted to learn everything he could. George would later become a professor. He taught at the Tuskegee Institute in Alabama. Even as an adult, he continued to love learning about everything he could.

One of the things George loved learning about the most was plants. He loved science and enjoyed learning all he could about how plants grew. The school where George taught had a farm. George was allowed to plant crops on the farm and study the plants that were grown there.

George noticed the cotton the farm tried to grow was not doing well. He told everyone the land needed to rest. He and his students tried something new. They decided to plant a different crop. For two years, they grew different crops. On the third year, they grew cotton again. The cotton did very well because the land had rested.

The soil where the cotton was planted was doing very well. However, the crop now had another problem. The cotton was being eaten by a bug called a boll weevil. Boll weevils love cotton. George had another idea. Instead of planting cotton, he told the school to plant peanuts. Boll weevils hate peanuts. The peanuts did well, but no one knew what to do with a crop of peanuts.

George did not give up. He worked with the peanuts to find many ways to use them. He used the peanuts to make bread, soup, cookies, and even ice cream. The food the people seemed to love the most was the peanut butter he made.

George Washington Carver was a friend to the farmers. He was also a great scientist and inventor. He helped farmers learn better ways to use their soil. He also made the peanut a food that nearly everyone could use.

The following pages have questions based on the texts from Unit 15.
You may look at the stories to help answer any questions. Use the
back of the page if you need extra space for writing your answers.

1 Which word could be used as a synonym for the word *harvested* as it is used in the
following sentence?

Peanuts are harvested in the fall.

(a) sold

(b) gathered

(c) cooked

(d) shelled

2 Which adjective best describes George Washington Carver?

(a) sneaky

(b) silly

(c) clever

(d) angry

3 What happened after George planted peanuts at the farm?

(a) He went to teach in Alabama.

(b) He became a slave.

(c) He planted different crops at the farm.

(d) He invented many different ways to use peanuts.

4 List two ways George used peanuts.

a. _____

_____

b. _____

_____

5 Where does Joy find the peanuts she will eat?

(a) on the leaves of the plant   (c) at the tip of the leaf

(b) in the soil   (d) on the vine of the plant

6   What does the author mean when he or she says "George had a passion for education"?

(a) He did not like to learn.

(b) He could not read.

(c) He wanted to learn to read.

(d) He liked learning about different things.

7   What do the two characters in each text have in common?

(a) They both live in Alabama.

(b) They both like to go to school.

(c) They both enjoy planting crops.

(d) They both have small families.

8   Which statement is a fact?

(a) Peanuts are the best crop because they can be used for many things.

(b) Everyone should plant peanuts.

(c) Boll weevils hate peanuts.

(d) George Washington Carver was the best teacher who ever lived.

9   What did Joy do with the spade?

(a) She opened the shells of the peanuts.

(b) She dug the peanuts out from the soil.

(c) She planted new peanut plants.

(d) She cut off leaves.

10 Write the sentence from the text that helped you to answer #9.

_____

_____

_____

_____

Time to Write!

Imagine you are writing a letter to George Washington Carver. You want him to try planting a new food at his farm.

1. Choose the food you want to be planted.

2. Explain why you want him to try this plant at his farm.

3. Tell him all the wonderful things that can be done with the food from this plant.

4. Offer to help him plant the new crop.

Use the space below to write your letter.

Dear Mr. George Washington Carver,

_____

_____

_____

_____

_____

_____

_____

_____

_____

_____

Sincerely,

_____

A Place on the Wall

"Dan, you need to be neater."

Dan knew his mother was right.
He looked at the writing on his
paper. It looked messy. He wished
his letters looked as good the ones
from the other students in his class.
He wasn't sure what he could do to
make his writing look better.

"Bring your paper over to the table,"
Dan's mother said. "I will help you redo your page.
Maybe together we can make it look better."

Dan brightened up at this idea. He knew his mother would help him find a
way to make the work look better. She always had great ideas. She was a good
teacher just like his classroom teacher, Mrs. Melton.

Dan's mother placed a new sheet of paper in front of him. She made sure he
had a sharp pencil to use for his writing. She told him to sit up straight. She
showed him how to hold his pencil. Then she went over to the computer. Dan
heard the printer come to life. His mother came back with the alphabet printed
on a piece of paper.

"Think about what you want to write. Then look at each letter carefully," his
mother said. "Remember, being neat shows you care about the work you do."

Dan took his time on his work. He tried to do everything his mother asked him
to do. He wanted his mother and his teacher to be proud of his work.

The next day, he turned in his work to his teacher.

"Dan, this is the best handwriting I have ever seen you do. I am going to hang
your paper on the wall for everyone to see," she said.

Dan was so happy. His teacher was proud of his work. His mother would be
proud of his work, and Dan was proud, too.

The Art of Writing

When people write, they can put their ideas on paper. The ideas they write down can always be remembered. Learning how to write is an important skill. Of course, most people learn to talk long before they learn how to write. However, learning to write is just as important as talking.

Long ago, people drew pictures on the walls of caves. These pictures were a way to tell their stories. This was some of the earliest forms of writing. Today, people can type their words using an electronic device such as a tablet, a computer, and even a phone. There are many ways to write down ideas using technology. Even with technology, it is still important for people to know how to write on paper.

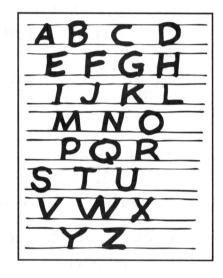

Most young people learn two styles of handwriting. Children first learn to print their letters. This print writing is called manuscript writing. Children's books are usually written in manuscript letters. Students are used to seeing these letters in the books they read.

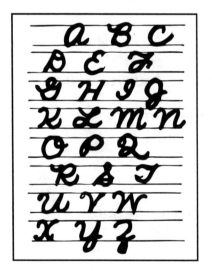

Once a student has learned to print, he or she can learn to make cursive letters. When a student learns to make cursive letters, he or she can usually write faster. With cursive letters, the writer leaves his or her pencil on the paper. The letters are all joined by small loops. A writer does not lift his or her pencil off the paper until he or she has finished a word. Many people write using both print and cursive letters.

Writing is important. People use writing to share ideas with others. Ideas that are written can last for hundreds of years!

The following pages have questions based on the texts from Unit 16. You may look at the stories to help answer any questions. Use the back of the page if you need extra space for writing your answers.

1 What does the prefix "re–" mean in this sentence?

I will help you redo your page.

    (a) same

    (b) not

    (c) again

    (d) before

2 What does the suffix "–er" mean in this sentence?

"Dan, you need to be neater."

    (a) most

    (b) less

    (c) more

    (d) not

3 From the text "The Art of Writing," how did some people first begin to write?

    (a) They wrote letters with ink and a feather.

    (b) They drew pictures in the sand.

    (c) They wrote with pen and paper.

    (d) They drew pictures on the walls of caves.

4 Write the sentence from the text that helped you to answer #3.

_____

_____

_____

5 What do the two stories have in common?

_____

_____

_____

6 What is an example of something that would not exist if people could not write?

_____

_____

7 Which is an advantage of writing cursive letters instead of print letters?

(a) Cursive letters are easier to write.

(b) Cursive letters are faster to write.

(c) Cursive letters are prettier.

(d) Cursive letters can be read by everyone.

8 Why does Dan's mother make a copy of the letters of the alphabet?

(a) so Dan can see how to write the letters

(b) so she can see what the letters look like

(c) so Dan can take the letters to his teacher

(d) so Dan can practice tracing the letters

9 In the story "The Art of Writing," which is a true statement?

(a) Most children learn to print their letters first.

(b) Most children learn to write cursive letters first.

(c) Most children should not learn to write on paper.

(d) Most children should never write on a computer.

10 Why does Dan's mother tell Dan he should be neater with his work?

_____

_____

_____

_____

Time to Write!

Use your best handwriting to complete the activity below.

Write in print or cursive. Write a paragraph telling about something you have always wished you could have.

- Explain what you want.

- List at least three reasons why you want it.

- Tell how you can get it or why you can't get it.

_____

_____

_____

_____

_____

_____

_____

_____

_____

_____

_____

_____

_____

_____

_____

In the News

"I want to join the school newspaper," Maddie told her teacher.

Mr. Jackson took off his glasses and looked at Maddie. Mr. Jackson was in charge of the school paper. He could tell Maddie if she could or could not write for the paper. Maddie waited for his answer.

"That sounds like a great idea, Maddie," he said. "What type of stories do you want to write?"

Maddie was so happy Mr. Jackson was going to let her write for the paper. She had thought a lot about what she would write. She loved reading the school's paper. She liked all of the stories that were in the paper. She wanted to write something different than everyone else.

"I would like to interview the teachers," Maddie told Mr. Jackson. "Everyone always interviews the students. No one ever interviews the teachers. They are a part of the school, too."

Mr. Jackson nodded his head. Maddie could tell he liked her idea. "You are acting like a reporter already, Maddie. I am glad you are reading the paper. I am glad you see something that will help make the news better."

"If I can start today, I would like to interview you, Mr. Jackson."

Mr. Jackson laughed. "I am glad you are ready to get started. Okay, Maddie. You can interview me. Do you have your questions ready?"

Maddie pulled out her notebook and pencil. She had written her questions the night before. "Oh, I'm ready, Mr. Jackson. I am ready!"

Sequoyah

Sequoyah was born around 1760. He was born in East Tennessee. He was a Native American. He was one of the greatest Cherokee Indians who ever lived. When Sequoyah grew up, the Cherokee Indians did not have a system of writing. Sequoyah knew many things about the traditions of his people. He had no way to write down all the many things he knew. Writing down the traditions of the Cherokee Indians would help everyone remember them.

As Sequoyah grew older, he met many white settlers. Sequoyah wanted to know more about the way the settlers wrote things down. The Cherokee people did not have an alphabet. He wanted to learn all he could about the way people wrote.

Sequoyah decided to make an alphabet for his people. He worked hard to make this happen. After twelve years, he had a system of writing for his people. His system was perfect for the Cherokee language.

Sequoyah was happy with his work. He knew his people could write down their traditions. He wanted the tribe's important information to be saved in writing. Sequoyah's alphabet would also be used to write books and newspapers. The Cherokee people could now learn to read and write in their own language.

Sequoyah was respected by many people. He was a great help to his own tribe. Later in his life, he went to Washington D.C. to speak. He wanted to speak for many of the Indians. Things did not always go the way Sequoyah hoped they would go. Still, Sequoyah was able to make a huge difference in the lives of many of his Native-American friends.

The following pages have questions based on the texts from Unit 17. You may look at the stories to help answer any questions. Use the back of the page if you need extra space for writing your answers.

1 What do both texts have in common?

(a) Both explain how going to school is important.

(b) Both are about Native Americans.

(c) Both explain how important writing is.

(d) Both are about making an alphabet.

2 Write one fact from the text "Sequoyah."

_____

_____

_____

3 Write one opinion from the text "Sequoyah."

_____

_____

_____

4 Who are the characters in the story "In the News"?

a. _____

b. _____

5 How did Sequoyah most likely feel about creating a system of writing for the Cherokee Indians?

(a) nervous

(b) proud

(c) angry

(d) shy

6 What is Maddie's idea?

ⓐ She wants to interview the students.

ⓑ She wants to interview the principal.

ⓒ She wants to interview the parents.

ⓓ She wants to interview the teachers.

7 Why did Sequoyah want to make a Cherokee alphabet?

ⓐ He wanted the Cherokee people to be able to write in their own language.

ⓑ He wanted to start a newspaper.

ⓒ He wanted to be a famous author.

ⓓ He wanted to go to Washington D.C.

8 Which word could be used to describe both Maddie and Sequoyah?

ⓐ rude

ⓑ silly

ⓒ determined

ⓓ cheerful

9 What is one reason people might want to write something down instead of just remembering it?

_____

_____

_____

10 Why does Maddie think it is important to interview the teachers?

_____

_____

_____

Time to Write!

Use the outline below to make your own school newspaper page.

1. Make a title for your school paper in box 1.

2. Write a short article about your teacher or your principal in box 2.

3. Draw and color a picture of something at your school in box 3.

4. Write a longer story about yourself in box 4. Be sure to tell about things you do at your school.

Making a Difference

Alice held tightly to her mother's hand. There were a lot of people at the school. Alice thought that was funny because school was over for the day.

"Mom," Alice said, tugging on her mother's arm. "Why are we at my school? Why are all these people here?"

"Today is an election day. Your school is where I come to vote each time there is an election," her mother explained. "Voting machines are set up in the school's library."

The doors opened to the library, and Alice and her mother walked inside. Alice's mother showed a man a small card. Alice's mother explained that the card said she was able to vote in the election. Alice told her mother she wanted a card, too. Alice's mother laughed.

"Someday, Alice, you can have your own card. You are too young to vote now. We are lucky to be able to vote. When we vote, we are able to help make important decisions about the government. Some countries do not let their citizens vote."

Alice nodded. She remembered her teacher talking about how important voting was. Her teacher had also told the class that women had not always had the right to vote. That was hard for Alice to imagine.

Alice watched her mother go up to the voting machine. She did not know whom she was voting for, but that did not matter to Alice. At that moment, she was proud of her mother just for voting. She understood that what her mother was doing was very important.

Someday, Alice thought, *I will be able to vote for myself.* When Alice's mother finished voting, Alice told her what she had been thinking.

"Who knows?" Alice's mother said. "Someday you may even be the person everyone is voting for!"

Fighting for Suffrage

Did you know there was a time when women were not allowed to vote? Even though women were American citizens, they were not given the right to vote. In the 1800s, some women thought this was okay. However, some women did not agree with the way women were treated. They believed women should have the same rights as men. They believed women should have suffrage. The word *suffrage* means the right to vote.

One person who spoke up for women was Susan B. Anthony. She was born in Massachusetts in 1820. When she grew up, she became a teacher. She also began speaking out for the rights of women. Susan thought women should have equal pay. She also thought women should be given the right to vote. If women could vote, she thought that America could change for the better. One thing Susan wanted to change was slavery. She thought slavery was wrong.

Susan began to speak up for women. She would travel all over and give speeches for women to have more rights in America. Not everyone agreed with everything Susan had to say. Some women thought she was wrong! Susan, however, did not give up. People began to listen to her speeches. Other people began to believe as she did.

Susan B. Anthony died in 1906. She was never able to vote. Women in America were not allowed to vote until 1919. In 1919, the 19th amendment was passed. This amendment to the Constitution gave women the right to vote. Susan B. Anthony may have never voted, but she helped other women have the right to vote. Because she never gave up, women in America now have a chance to be heard.

The United States wanted to honor Susan for all she did for women. In 1979, an image of Susan B. Anthony was placed on the dollar coin. She was the first woman to ever be on American money.

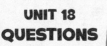
Name	Date

The following pages have questions based on the texts from Unit 18. You may look at the stories to help answer any questions. Use the back of the page if you need extra space for writing your answers.

1 What do both texts have in common?

(a) Both are about mothers and daughters.

(b) Both are about women being able to vote.

(c) Both are about how to vote.

(d) Both are about Susan B. Anthony.

2 What will Alice most likely do once she grows up?

(a) never vote

(b) vote

(c) forget to ever vote

(d) try and talk people into not voting

3 Why was Susan B. Anthony's image put on a coin?

(a) She helped get women the right to vote.

(b) She was a wonderful teacher.

(c) She was the first woman president.

(d) She ended slavery.

4 What does the word *suffrage* mean?

(a) to be able to speak

(b) to be able to vote

(c) to be able to teach

(d) to be able to sing

5 Write the sentence from the text "Fighting for Suffrage" that helped you to answer #4.

_____

_____

_____

_____

6 What can you tell about Alice from reading the story "Making a Difference"?

  (a) She is proud of her mother.

  (b) She hopes her father will vote.

  (c) She wants to grow up to be the president.

  (d) She wants to be a teacher like Susan B. Anthony.

7 Write the sentence from the story that helped you to answer #6.

_____

_____

_____

_____

8 Give one reason why Alice's mother might need a special card to be able to vote.

_____

_____

_____

9 Which would be a good alternative title for the text "Making a Difference"?

  (a) "A Day with Mom"

  (b) "Back at School"

  (c) "Learning to Vote"

  (d) "The Small Card"

10 Which sentence is true?

  (a) Susan B. Anthony was the first woman to vote.

  (b) Susan B. Anthony was never able to vote.

  (c) Susan B. Anthony didn't want women to have the right to vote.

  (d) Susan B. Anthony only wanted men to be able to vote.

Time to Write!

Part 1

Have you ever wondered why children can't vote? Maybe children should be able to vote. Think about all the reasons people under the age of 18 should be able to vote.

Now, list three reasons why children should have the right to vote.

1. _____

_____

2. _____

_____

3. _____

_____

Part 2

On second thought, maybe there is a reason children can't vote. Think about why children aren't able to vote.

Now, list three reasons why children should NOT have the right to vote.

1. _____

_____

2. _____

_____

3. _____

_____

Something Extra: On the back of the page, draw and color a poster showing that children should be able to vote.

"Hurry, children. It's almost time to go!"

Nancy took one last look in the mirror. She liked her costume. She was a cat for Halloween. Her shirt and pants were both black. Her mother had made ears to go on her headband and a tail to pin to her back. She had drawn a black nose and whiskers on her face.

Nancy turned to help her little sister finish putting on her wings. Kat was a fairy. Kat was a fairy every year. She never wanted a different costume. She thought Kat should have wanted to be a cat. Nancy had to admit that Kat made a very cute fairy. She just didn't understand why she never wanted to try something new. Why couldn't she be an angel or even a butterfly? They both had wings. The two girls ran down the stairs. Their mother and father were waiting for them.

"You two look very scary," their father said.

"Oh, Daddy," Kat laughed. "Why do I have to tell you every Halloween? Fairies aren't scary."

"Can cats be scary?" he asked Nancy.

Nancy nodded her head. She liked the idea of being a scary cat; she just didn't want to be a scaredy cat. There would be lots of ghosts and goblins out on Halloween. She didn't want any of the other children's costumes to scare her.

The girls' mother handed each one a bag for their treats. They were just about to leave when their father turned around and stopped.

"Wait!"

"What's wrong, Daddy?" both girls asked at the same time.

"You are both forgetting something." The two girls did not know what he meant. Then he pulled out a big bowl of treats. "You forgot to say 'trick or treat' at your very first house!"

It took the girls less than a second to say the magic words.

A Spooky Night

Many years ago, some people celebrated the start of the new year on a different day than we do today. Long ago, some groups of people celebrated November 1 as the first day of the year. They called this special day All Souls Day. They believed the night before All Souls Day was a special day, too. They thought that on October 31, the world of the living and the land of the dead could mix.

They called this night All Hallow's Eve. People believed ghosts could come out on this night. They would light huge bonfires to keep away evil spirits. People also cut scary faces into pumpkins to keep away bad things. Today, we call these pumpkins jack-o'-lanterns. Today, we celebrate Halloween on October 31.

Trick-or-treating is another fun part of Halloween. No one knows for sure how trick-or-treating began. In the United States, most children did not start going door to door for candy until after World War II.

The idea to go trick-or-treating began to show up in magazines and cartoons. People also started wearing costumes for Halloween. Both children and adults enjoy dressing up for this celebration.

Today, there are many fun things to do on Halloween. Some people have cookouts. Other people have hayrides. Still, others like to go to haunted houses. The best part of Halloween is just being with friends and family and having fun. Even if you do not like to go trick-or-treating, it is fun to see what costumes everyone is wearing. You never know who will come to your door on Halloween night. You might see a ghost. You might come across a pirate. You might even see a witch! But, if you're really lucky, your Halloween holiday will be all treats and no tricks!

The following pages have questions based on the texts from Unit 19. You may look at the stories to help answer any questions. Use the back of the page if you need extra space for writing your answers.

1 Which sentence from "Trick or Treat" has a compound word?

(a) She had drawn a black nose and whiskers on her face.

(b) Why couldn't she be an angel or even a butterfly?

(c) The girls' mother handed each one a bag for their treats.

(d) It took the girls less than a second to say the magic words.

2 Which sentence is NOT true?

(a) Some people used to celebrate November 1 as the first day of the year.

(b) People cut faces into pumpkins to scare away evil spirits.

(c) People have always gone trick-or-treating on Halloween.

(d) Today, Halloween is celebrated on October 31.

3 Put the three events in order. Write each letter on the correct line.

    a. Nancy and Kat got treats at their house.

    b. Nancy and Kat finished putting on their costumes

    c. Nancy and Kat ran down the stairs of their house.

      1st _____   **2nd** _____   **3rd** _____

4 What costume did Kat always wear?

(a) a cat costume

(b) a butterfly costume

(c) an angel costume

(d) a fairy costume

5 What do the two texts have in common?

_____

_____

_____

6 What did Kat and Nancy forget to do?

    (a) They forgot to put on Kat's wings.

    (b) They forgot to draw whiskers on Nancy's face.

    (c) They forgot to wait for their parents.

    (d) They forgot to go trick-or-treating at their own house.

7 Which sentence from the story helped you to answer #6?

_____

_____

_____

_____

8 Which statement is a fact about Halloween?

    (a) Halloween is fun because everyone gets candy.

    (b) Halloween is a very scary holiday.

    (c) Halloween is always on October 31.

    (d) Halloween should be everyone's favorite holiday.

9 Why did people light fires on All Hallows' Eve?

    (a) to stay warm

    (b) to use for cooking

    (c) to have more light

    (d) to keep away evil spirits

10 Write the sentence from the text that helped you to answer #9.

_____

_____

_____

_____

Time to Write!

All holidays start somewhere. Imagine you get to create your very own holiday! Use the space below to help make your special day happen.

What is the name of your new holiday?

_____

When is your new holiday?

_____

What do you do on your holiday?

_____

_____

_____

What makes your holiday special?

_____

_____

_____

Do you give or get gifts on your holiday? Explain your answer.

_____

_____

_____

Who celebrates your new holiday and why?

_____

_____

_____

Something New

Lisa had never been to her grandparents' house. They lived far away from her own house. She talked to them on the phone. They came and visited her. They wrote letters back and forth. Tonight was the first time, though, that Lisa had been to their house. Lisa's parents had agreed to let her fly on an airplane all by herself to Kentucky. When she stepped off the plane, one of the people from the airport had stayed with her until she had found her grandparents. Lisa had been a little scared, but she had been more excited than anything else. She was going to spend two weeks with her grandparents. She couldn't wait!

"Well, does the house look like what you had imagined?" Lisa's grandmother asked her as they walked through the front door.

Lisa nodded her head. She had seen pictures of the outside. She had only imagined the inside from what her grandmother had told her on the phone. It wasn't exactly the same, but it was warm and cozy just like she knew it would be.

"I think you need to call your parents now so they don't worry," her grandfather said. Lisa was surprised. She told her grandparents that she thought they had already called her parents from the airport.

"We couldn't call from there," her grandmother explained. "We don't have a cell phone." Lisa knew that. She had just forgotten. She wondered how her grandmother called their house.

Her grandmother walked Lisa to the kitchen. She pointed to the phone. It was a large, black phone. It was hanging from the wall. Lisa had never seen a phone like this before. Her grandmother picked up part of the phone and held it to Lisa's ear. The rest of the phone stayed on the wall. A cord with curls kept both pieces together. She watched as her grandmother put her finger into small holes beside the numbers. She moved her finger in a half circle to dial each one. It seemed to take a long time for her grandmother to dial the numbers.

Lisa couldn't wait to tell her parents about everything, including the unusual phone she was using to call them.

Changing Technology

Have you ever heard of Alexander Graham Bell? If you haven't heard of him, you still probably know his invention. Bell invented the telephone. Of course, the phone he invented looked much different than the phone you use today! The telephone can put people in contact with each other instantly. But how did people communicate over long distances before there were telephones?

A long time ago, people could not use computers or phones to talk to people far away. They had to have different ways to reach each other. Different animals were used to deliver messages. Some people actually used birds to carry messages. Certain types of birds were trained to carry messages back and forth. Someone would tie a small message to the leg of the bird. The bird was trained to carry the message back to a certain place. Dogs were also used to send letters. In areas with lots of snow, dogs would pull sleds. The sleds would have mail that needed to be sent to other places.

Horses were also used to send mail. The Pony Express was a system used out West. People would ride horses across the land and deliver the mail to places where trains could not go.

The invention of the telegraph helped people send messages even quicker than mail. Messages were sent across power lines. People used a special code to send their words across the lines. The telegraph operator would decode the message and then tell it to the person it was sent to.

Alexander Graham Bell's telephone let people talk across wires. Today's phones no longer use wires. They are sent through signals in the air. Communication is always getting better. Who knows how you will talk to someone far away in the future!

The following pages have questions based on the texts from Unit 20. You may look at the stories to help answer any questions. Use the back of the page if you need extra space for writing your answers.

1 Which sentence is the best summary of paragraph 1 of the story "Something New"?

   (a) Lisa was nervous about flying.

   (b) Lisa was homesick.

   (c) Lisa was going to visit her grandparents for the first time.

   (d) Lisa wanted to be an airline pilot when she grew up.

2 Who invented the telephone?

   (a) Abraham Lincoln

   (b) Thomas Edison

   (c) Lisa's grandfather

   (d) Alexander Graham Bell

3 Which sentence from the text "Changing Technology" helped you to answer #2?

_____

_____

_____

_____

4 Why did people most likely stop using animals to deliver messages?

_____

_____

_____

5 Why had Lisa never visited her grandparents' house?

   (a) She did not get along with her grandparents.

   (b) Her grandparents did not want her to come and visit.

   (c) She didn't want to leave her friends.

   (d) Her grandparents lived far away.

6 Which sentence contains a compound word?

(a) Lisa's parents had agreed to let her fly on an airplane all by herself to Kentucky.

(b) Lisa had been a little scared, but she had been more excited than anything else.

(c) She pointed to the phone.

(d) She moved her finger in a half circle to dial each one.

7 Which two words make up the compound word you found in #6?

a. _____

b. _____

8 What does the word *instantly* mean as it is used in the following sentence?

The telephone can put people in contact with each other instantly.

(a) later

(b) right away

(c) soon

(d) in the future

9 List two types of animals that helped deliver messages.

a. _____

b. _____

10 Write one way technology has changed.

_____

_____

_____

_____

_____

Time to Write!

There are many ways people can "talk" to each other. Using phone calls, email, and text are just some ways people communicate with each other. People also still write letters to each other.

Think of someone you would like to write a letter to. They can be someone far away or someone close to home. Use the space below to write a letter to that special someone.

Dear _____,

_____

_____

_____

_____

_____

_____

_____

_____

_____

_____

_____

                              _____

                              _____

Dear Diary

Sophie and her mother had been shopping all day. Her mother had bought Sophie many special things at the mall. She had two new outfits and one new pair of shoes. She had some new school supplies. And she had a new diary.

Sophie had never owned a diary. Her mother told her she'd had a diary when she was a little girl. She still had it. Sometimes, she would read what she had written. She told Sophie that pictures capture memories, but her diary would remind her about her thoughts. She hoped Sophie would fill her diary with her own special thoughts.

What Sophie liked best about her new diary was the tiny silver key. She liked that she could lock up her diary each day. Her little brother, Brian, was always getting into her things. This way she knew her diary would be safe from him. She decided to put the key in her jewelry box. The box was on her dresser. It was too high for Brian to reach.

That night, Sophie wrote three pages in her diary. She wrote all about her family. She wrote about her friends, too. She also decided to write about things that were going on in the world. She thought it would be fun to read her diary someday and see how things had changed.

Finally, Sophie was finished writing. After she had locked the diary and put away the key, she put the diary underneath her bed. She decided she would write each night in her diary. She couldn't wait to tell her mother how much she had already written.

History Through Writing

Many people in history have written in diaries or journals. Most probably never thought other people would see what they wrote. Some diaries have become very famous. The written pages tell people today what the world was like years ago.

One famous diary is Anne Frank's diary. Anne Frank was a young girl who lived during World War II. Anne and her family had to go into hiding during the war. While Anne was hiding, she kept a diary. She wrote down what life was like for her. She left her pages behind when her family was captured. Later, the pages from her diary were gathered together. Her words were published in a book. People all over the world have read Anne's words. Her diary has helped people everywhere wish for a world with no wars.

Helen Keller is another famous person who kept a journal. Helen Keller was born in Alabama in 1880. When she was nineteen months old, she became very sick. The illness left her blind and deaf. Because she could not hear, she did not learn to speak. Helen had been a very bright child, but no one knew how to teach her. Her family tried many different things to help her. Finally, they found Anne Sullivan. Anne came to Alabama in 1887. She became Helen's teacher. She was able to teach Helen by spelling words into her hands. Helen could now talk to others. She could now learn. In fact, Anne was such a wonderful teacher that Helen even graduated from college.

Anne stayed with Helen her entire life. When Anne died, Helen was very sad. She wrote in a journal about her feelings. Anne had been her best friend as well as her teacher. She missed her very much. She started writing in the journal just two weeks after Anne's death. The pages of her journal tell about their friendship and how much she missed her dear teacher.

UNIT 21 QUESTIONS

Name _____ **Date** _____

The following pages have questions based on the texts from Unit 21. You may look at the stories to help answer any questions. Use the back of the page if you need extra space for writing your answers.

1 Which sentence helps the reader know Sophie had never written in a diary?

   (a) She had some new school supplies.

   (b) Sophie had always owned a diary.

   (c) Her mother told her she'd had a diary when she was a little girl.

   (d) Sophie had never owned a diary.

2 Why does Sophie like having a key for her diary?

   (a) She has never owned a key.

   (b) She doesn't want her mother to read her diary.

   (c) She doesn't want her little brother to open her diary.

   (d) She likes the color of the key.

3 Using the text, write the name of one famous person who wrote a diary.

_____

4 Why did Helen Keller write in her journal?

   (a) She wanted to write about a trip she went on.

   (b) She wanted to write about her teacher and friend.

   (c) She wanted to write about growing up in Alabama.

   (d) She wanted to write about Anne Frank.

5 Which paragraph in "History Through Writing" helped you to answer #4?

   (a) paragraph 1

   (b) paragraph 2

   (c) paragraph 3

   (d) paragraph 4

6 Which sentence is an opinion?

  (a) Everyone should have a diary.

  (b) Helen Keller wrote in a journal.

  (c) Anne Frank lived during World War II.

  (d) Many people have had diaries.

7 Write three events that happened in order in the story "Dear Diary."

First, _____

_____

Next, _____

_____

Finally, _____

_____

8 How many pages did Sophie write in her diary the first night?

  (a) She did not write in her diary.

  (b) She wrote one page.

  (c) She wrote two pages.

  (d) She wrote three pages.

9 Write the sentence from the story that helped you to answer #8.

_____

_____

_____

10 Which sentence would be the best summary for the story "Dear Diary"?

  (a) Sophie was happy about getting a new diary.

  (b) Sophie loved going shopping with her mother.

  (c) Sophie wanted to write a famous diary.

  (d) Sophie did not like writing in a diary.

Time to Write!

Part 1

Imagine you could make a cover for your own diary. Use the space below to draw a cover for your book. Be sure to color the picture when you are done.

Part 2

Write the first page in your diary. Write about a day at school. Be sure to use lots of adjectives to describe your day.

Dear Diary,

Today I . . . _____

_____

_____

_____

_____

_____

_____

_____

Shark

Ben's family had planned their trip to the beach for over a year. He could not believe they were finally looking at the ocean. The white sand felt cool between his toes. His mother was already putting sunscreen on his little brother and sister. He knew he would be next. He didn't mind. He couldn't wait to go swimming.

When Ben stepped into the water, it felt warm. He was surprised. The water in the pool at home usually felt cold. His father was beside him as he went into the water. His brother and sister had stayed on the beach with his mother. They were more interested in building castles in the sand than getting into the water. That was okay with Ben. He knew the ocean was huge. His father wouldn't have to watch so many people if it were just the two of them.

Ben's father had brought a float into the water. They were both able to hang on to the float. They waited for a wave to build out in the water. Then they hopped onto the float. They would ride the waves into the shore. Then they would swim back out into the water and ride the waves again. Ben thought he could play in the water forever. He was having so much fun riding the waves with his father.

Ben and his father were ready to go back out into the water when they heard a whistle blow. They saw a lifeguard trying to get their attention. They turned away from the water and walked over to see what was wrong.

"I'm sorry," the lifeguard said, "but we need you to stay on the shore for a while."

"What's wrong?" Ben's father asked the lifeguard.

"We spotted a shark in the area where you were swimming," the lifeguard explained. "It would be better to stay out of the water for now." Ben and his father thanked the lifeguard for his help. Ben was glad they were at the beach, and it was fun to do new things, but he was not ready to meet a shark!

King of the Sea

Sharks are one of the predators of the ocean. They are carnivores. They feed on other animals of the sea. Sharks live in all types of oceans but are more common in warmer waters. Some sharks have even been found in lakes and rivers where the waters run out into the sea.

Sharks are an amazing kind of fish. There are many different types of sharks. The hammerhead shark has a flattened head that looks like the head of a hammer. The whale shark is the largest type of shark. The whale shark only eats smaller fish and plankton. This shark can grow to over forty feet long. Its weight can be as much as two African elephants! On the other hand, some sharks are very small. Some sharks are only six inches long. Can you imagine such a small shark?

People usually recognize a shark first by its dorsal fin. The dorsal fin is located on the back of the shark. It is often seen out of the water while the rest of the shark's body is underneath the water. The shark also has unusual teeth. A shark has more than one row of teeth. The shark loses old teeth. New teeth will continue to grow each time old teeth are lost. In some sharks, new teeth can grow back every week!

Sharks are amazing creatures. They are fast swimmers and skilled hunters. No one can argue that the shark is the king of the sea.

Hammerhead Shark

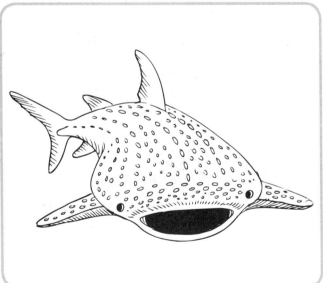

Whale Shark

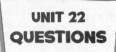
UNIT 22
QUESTIONS

Name

Date

The following pages have questions based on the texts from Unit 22. You may look at the stories to help answer any questions. Use the back of the page if you need extra space for writing your answers.

1 Which sentence is an opinion?

(a) Sharks are carnivores.

(b) Sharks live in all types of oceans but are more common in warmer waters.

(c) There are many different types of sharks.

(d) No one can argue that the shark is the king of the sea.

2 What do Ben's brother and sister want to do at the beach?

(a) go swimming

(b) take a nap

(c) play in the sand

(d) chase seagulls

3 What paragraph in the text helped you to answer #2?

(a) paragraph 1

(b) paragraph 2

(c) paragraph 3

(d) paragraph 4

4 Why do Ben and his father have to stay out of the water?

(a) Ben is not feeling well.

(b) Ben's father wants to take a nap.

(c) The lifeguard saw a shark.

(d) The lifeguard saw someone drowning.

5 Write a sentence explaining how Ben feels about being at the beach.

_____

_____

_____

_____

6 Which shark is the largest shark in the sea?

    (a) the hammerhead

    (b) the great white

    (c) the whale shark

    (d) the bull shark

7 In the text "King of the Sea," which paragraph helped you to answer #6?

    (a) paragraph 1

    (b) paragraph 2

    (c) paragraph 3

    (d) paragraph 4

8 What do the two texts have in common?

    (a) the ocean

    (b) sharks

    (c) whales

    (d) the beach

9 What does the word *carnivores* means as it is used in the following sentence?

They are carnivores.

    (a) They only eat plants.

    (b) They eat other animals.

    (c) They only eat seaweed.

    (d) They only eat other sharks.

10 Which sentence from the text helped you to answer #9?

_____

_____

_____

_____

Time to Write!

Part 1

Choose one of the ocean animals. Circle the one you choose.

clownfish	**octopus**	**starfish**
eel	**pufferfish**	**walrus**
jellyfish	**shrimp**	**whale**

Part 2

With the help of your teacher, research the animal you chose. Use the questions below to help with your research.

1. Where does your animal live? _____

   _____

2. What does your animal look like? _____

   _____

3. What does your animal eat? _____

   _____

4. What enemies does your animal have? _____

   _____

5. What size is your animal? _____

   _____

6. List at least one other unique fact you learned about your animal.

   _____

   _____

   _____

Something Extra: On the back of this page, draw and color a picture of your animal in its habitat.

Speaking Out

Kara wanted it to stop. Each morning at her school, a group of girls were always mean to some of the children in the lower grades. She had watched the girls shove the younger kids out of line. She had seen them knock their backpacks off their arms and then laugh.

She didn't know why they wanted to be mean, but she knew it was time to speak out. Things couldn't keep going the way they were. It was wrong for the girls to be bullies, but she knew it was wrong, too, for her to do nothing.

Mr. Kline was waiting for Kara to walk into the classroom. She had made herself be the last one in line because she wanted to talk to her teacher without anyone else around. As she got to the door, Mr. Kline greeted her. "Hello, Kara. How are you today?"

Kara knew that now was the time to speak up. She told him about the girls who were being bullies. She also told Mr. Kline that she had been scared to talk to him. She did not want the girls to be angry with her. Kara felt terrible that she had not spoken up before.

"I am proud of you, Kara," Mr. Kline told her. "You are standing up to bullies. If everyone would stand up to people who do the wrong thing, the world would be a better place. I will make sure this stops. I will also make sure the bullies understand why what they are doing is wrong so maybe they can change, too."

As Kara walked into the room, she felt better than she had in days. She knew now it was hard to speak up against things that were wrong, but it was the right thing to do. She hoped she would always be brave enough to do the right thing.

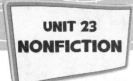

Having a Dream

Martin Luther King, Jr., is famous for speaking up for the rights of others. On August 28, 1963, Dr. King spoke to a huge crowd in Washington D.C. More than 200,000 people were there to hear him speak. His voice rang out loud and clear to those listening. His speech was about a dream he had for a country where everyone would be treated the same. His message was an important one. People listening to him were amazed to hear such a great speaker.

Why were there so many people in Washington D.C. that day? The people were there for the March on Washington. They wanted their voices to be heard by the president and other people in Washington. They wanted all people to be treated fairly.

Many parts of Dr. King's speech are remembered even today. Dr. King reminded others that the Declaration of Independence said that all men were created equal. If all men were equal, then all men should be treated the same. Dr. King also said many times that he had a dream for America. He had hopes that America would be a better country where everyone could live as equal citizens.

Dr. King's speech made a difference. It was one of the best speeches ever given. Because of his words, laws began to change. People began to be treated the same. He was brave and stood up and spoke up for others. Today, we celebrate Dr. King's life each January. Martin Luther King Day is a holiday to remember Dr. King's birth and life.

UNIT 23 QUESTIONS

Name _____ **Date** _____

The following pages have questions based on the texts from Unit 23. You may look at the stories to help answer any questions. Use the back of the page if you need extra space for writing your answers.

1 Which sentence is the best summary of the text "Having a Dream"?

   (a) We celebrate Dr. King's birthday each January.

   (b) Dr. King's speech in Washington D.C. made a difference in helping everyone be treated fairly.

   (c) Washington D.C. is a great place to take a vacation.

   (d) The March on Washington had more than 200,000 people.

2 What do the two texts have in common?

   (a) Both are about speaking up for others.

   (b) Both are about Dr. King.

   (c) Both are about bullying in schools.

   (d) Both are about dreams.

3 Which sentence is an opinion?

   (a) It was one of the best speeches ever given.

   (b) Dr. King spoke to a huge crowd in Washington D.C.

   (c) More than 200,000 people were there to hear him speak.

   (d) Martin Luther King Day is a holiday to remember Dr. King's birth and life.

4 Why is Kara afraid to talk to her teacher?

   (a) She is scared of Mr. Kline.

   (b) She doesn't know Mr. Kline.

   (c) She is scared the girls will be mad at her.

   (d) She is not afraid.

5 Which sentence from the story helped you to answer #4?

_____

_____

_____

6 Which happened first in the story?

    (a) Kara talks to Mr. Kline.

    (b) Kara is glad she spoke to Mr. Kline.

    (c) Kara sees the younger children being bullied.

    (d) Kara is the last person in line.

7 What does Kara have in common with Dr. King?

    (a) They both spoke up for others.

    (b) They are both from the same state.

    (c) They have both been to Washington D.C.

    (d) They both have birthdays in January.

8 Why does Kara most likely feel better after she talks to Mr. Kline?

    (a) She knows she did the right thing.

    (b) She likes talking to Mr. Kline.

    (c) She thought Mr. Kline was mad at her.

    (d) Mr. Kline gave her a special project to do.

9 What is the effect of Kara talking to Mr. Kline?

    (a) She will earn an A in his class.

    (b) The bullying will stop.

    (c) Mr. Kline will give Kara a test.

    (d) Kara will not have to ride the bus.

10 What was one effect of Dr. King's speech?

_____

_____

_____

_____

Time to Write!

Think of something you really care about. Maybe you think people should recycle. Maybe you want to stop bullying. Maybe you think animals should be treated better. Maybe you think the school needs a better playground.

Once you decide on a topic, use the space below to write a short speech to convince people to feel the same way you do about your topic.

Eating Worms

"I don't want to eat it," Vicky said. "It looks like worms." Vicky was not happy with the food on her plate. She had wanted pizza for supper. Vicky's mother had made spaghetti. Vicky had never tried spaghetti. She did not want to try it. She thought the noodles looked like slimy worms. All she could think about were the worms she saw each time after it rained. They would work their way out of the earth. They would wiggle and squiggle on the ground.

Her mother told her she would love the new food if she would just give it a try. Vicky knew her mother would not lie to her, but she still wasn't sure about eating it.

Jack, Vicky's brother, was already eating his second bowl. "Vicky, it's delicious," Jack told his sister. She watched him slurp up two noodles that were hanging from his mouth. He grinned as he made a slurp, slurp sound. Vicky thought it looked as though he was slurping up a long, slippery worm into his mouth.

"I have an idea," Jack said after he'd swallowed his big bite of food. "Why don't you close your eyes when you take your first bite? Then you won't see what you're eating!"

Vicky thought about Jack's words. For once, she thought her brother might actually have a good idea. All of her family liked spaghetti. Maybe if she could just try it without looking. But how would she keep her eyes closed?

Jack had an idea for that, too. He took one of the cloth napkins and tied it around her eyes. Now she couldn't see. Her mother took her hand and put her fingers around her fork. She dipped her fork into the spaghetti. She brought the fork up to her mouth. Slowly, slowly, she took a bite and swallowed.

She put down her fork and took off her blindfold. Then she looked at her family and smiled.

Maybe the "worms" weren't so bad after all!

A New Treat to Eat

Not all people eat the same foods. Some people eat meat. Some people only eat vegetables. Some people eat both. And some people eat bugs. That's right, some people eat bugs.

In many parts of the world, people eat insects as part of their daily meals. Grasshoppers, spiders, wasps, and even crickets are all on some people's list of foods to eat. Why would people eat insects? Well, for one thing there are lots of insects. Since there are a lot of insects, there would always be plenty of food. It takes a lot of land to raise livestock such as cows or pigs. Insects take up very little space compared to larger animals. Since insects take up very little space, more people could raise them. More people could grow their own food or even grow and sell the tasty treats. Eating insects could help feed billions of people!

Insects can also be a healthy food for people to eat. Many have protein and vitamins. People who have eaten insects say they often have a nutty taste. Creative cooks can add other ingredients and make the insects have many different flavors. What could be yummier than a chocolate-covered grasshopper?

Everyone might not be sold on the idea of eating bugs instead of cereal for breakfast. Many people have a hard time thinking about eating bugs. If they could try a yummy dish made with edible insects, they might just find a new treat to eat each week.

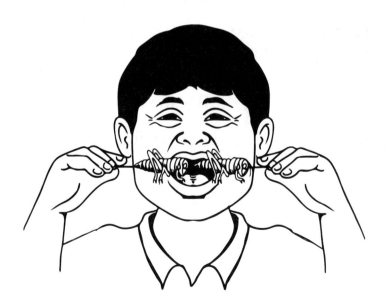

The following pages have questions based on the texts from Unit 24. You may look at the stories to help answer any questions. Use the back of the page if you need extra space for writing your answers.

1 Why does Vicky not want to try spaghetti?

    ⓐ She does not like trying new things.

    ⓑ She does not like spaghetti noodles.

    ⓒ She wanted pizza for supper.

    ⓓ She does not like the way the spaghetti looks.

2 Which part of the story best helped you to answer #1?

    ⓐ paragraph 1

    ⓑ paragraph 2

    ⓒ paragraph 3

    ⓓ the title

3 What is one reason why people might want to eat insects?

_____

_____

_____

4 What do some people say insects taste like?

    ⓐ chicken

    ⓑ nuts

    ⓒ chocolate

    ⓓ fruit

5 Which sentence from "A New Treat to Eat" helped you to answer #4?

_____

_____

_____

_____

6 What great idea did Jack have?

    ⓐ to fix Vicky something different to eat

    ⓑ to cover Vicky's eyes while she ate

    ⓒ to throw away the spaghetti

    ⓓ to take Vicky out to eat

7 What do the two texts have in common?

_____

_____

_____

8 Which sentence would be the best theme of the story "Eating Worms"?

    ⓐ Don't be afraid to try something new.

    ⓑ A good friend is hard to find.

    ⓒ Everyone is special.

    ⓓ You should always try your hardest.

9 What does the word *edible* mean as it is used in the following sentence?

If they could try a yummy dish made with edible insects, they might just find a new treat to eat each week.

    ⓐ something that cannot be eaten

    ⓑ something that should not be eaten

    ⓒ something that has never been eaten

    ⓓ something that can be eaten

10 If Vicky's family has spaghetti again for supper, what will Vicky most likely do?

    ⓐ She will find something else to eat.

    ⓑ She will eat the spaghetti.

    ⓒ She will ask her mother if they can go out to eat.

    ⓓ She will put a blindfold over her eyes before she eats.

Time to Write!

Part 1

Think about a food you tried that was new or different.

1. What did you try? _____

2. Why did you try it? _____

   _____

3. How did it taste? _____

   _____

4. What is something you have never eaten that you would like to try?

   _____

Part 2

Pretend you have been asked to make a new recipe. You have to prepare a dish in which the main ingredient is worms! What will you call your tasty new dish?

Now, use the recipe card below to write down all the ingredients. Be sure to write down the steps to cook your new dish.

Recipe for: _____

Ingredients

-
-
-
-

Steps to Make It

_____

_____

_____

_____

Playing the Game

Chase saw the ball coming. He was ready. The ball was about to go past him. He reached out with his hands and caught the ball before it could go by him. He looked at his coach. He knew what he would say. "I know, Coach. I know. I can't catch the ball in soccer," Chase said.

"That's right, Chase," his coach agreed. "I know it's hard to get used to, but you can't use your hands when you are going down the field."

Chase had played basketball for the past two years. He was used to making passes. He was used to catching the ball. He was used to using his hands to throw the ball through the hoop. Soccer was different than playing basketball. He really liked the game, though. He liked learning something new. He just didn't want to make a mistake during a game, and he didn't want to let his coach down. He also didn't want to let his team down.

"You're doing great, Chase." The coach encouraged him and then threw the ball right at Chase. Chase barely had time to think. He didn't catch the ball. Instead, he took a step back and stopped the ball with his body. Then he used his feet to move the ball. He passed the ball to another player on his team. He ran down the field. The ball was passed back to him. He was close to the goal. He lined up for a shot. He kicked the ball into the goal. He had scored! Even though it was only practice, Chase was grinning from ear to ear.

Everyone cheered. It was Chase's first goal.

"I knew you could do it," the coach said to Chase.

"Thanks," Chase replied. "I know I still have a lot to learn, but learning is really a lot of fun!"

Soccer

Soccer is a game that many people today enjoy playing and watching. Players have a lot of fun dribbling a soccer ball down the field. In some countries, the game is called "football" instead of "soccer." In the United States, football is a different sport. Football in the United States doesn't even use the same type of ball.

The game of soccer has some very basic rules. In a regular game, there are eleven players. One of these eleven players is the goalkeeper. The goalkeeper's job is to keep the other team's ball out of the net. If the ball goes into the net, the team scores one point. The goalkeeper is the one player who can use his hands. He can use his hands to stop the ball from going into the net. If the ball goes out of play, a player can also use his hands to throw the ball back onto the field. This is called a throw-in. The player who throws the ball back into play must keep both feet on the ground. He holds the ball in both hands. He puts the ball over his head. Then he throws the ball back onto the field, so the game can continue.

Both boys and girls play soccer. Children's teams can have boys and girls playing soccer together. If someone is very good at soccer, then they can play the game as their job. A person must be very talented and work very hard to become a professional soccer player. The biggest sporting event in soccer is the World Cup. The World Cup is a special sporting event because countries from all over the world play. Thirty-two teams compete in the World Cup. This special soccer event happens every four years.

The following pages have questions based on the texts from Unit 25. You may look at the stories to help answer any questions. Use the back of the page if you need extra space for writing your answers.

1 Which sentence contains a compound word?

   (a) Chase saw the ball coming.

   (b) Chase had played basketball for the past two years.

   (c) He passed the ball to another player on his team.

   (d) "I knew you could do it," the coach said to Chase.

2 Which two words make up the compound word from #1?

   a. _____

   b. _____

3 What do the two texts have in common?

   (a) They are both about soccer.

   (b) They are both about good coaches.

   (c) They are both about winning games.

   (d) They are both about never giving up.

4 Which would be a good alternative title for the text "Playing the Game"?

   (a) "Going, Going, Gone"

   (b) "Trying Something New"

   (c) "The Best Coach Ever"

   (d) "Basketball, Baseball, and Soccer"

5 What mistake does Chase make at practice?

   (a) He doesn't listen to the coach.

   (b) He won't share the ball.

   (c) He catches the ball with his hands.

   (d) He forgets to pass the ball.

6   Which statement is a fact?

    (a) Only girls can play soccer.

    (b) Both girls and boys can play soccer.

    (c) Soccer is only played in England.

    (d) Very few people enjoy playing soccer.

7   What other name is soccer sometimes called?

    (a) baseball

    (b) basketball

    (c) football

    (d) tennis

8   Write the sentence that helped you to answer #7.

_____

_____

_____

_____

9   What is the main purpose of the text "Soccer"?

    (a) to entertain

    (b) to persuade

    (c) to inform

    (d) to argue

10   Which word best describes Chase?

    (a) angry

    (b) silly

    (c) determined

    (d) shy

Time to Write!

Part 1

Many people enjoy playing soccer. What do you enjoy doing? Think about all the things you like to do. Write the things you enjoy doing on the white hexagon spaces below.

Part 2

Choose one of the things you wrote in Part 1. Then use the lines below to explain why you enjoy doing this thing.

_____

_____

_____

_____

The Lesson

"But I don't want to go to school," Abe told his mother. "Why can't it be Saturday every day?" Abe pulled the covers of his bed up over his head. His mother pulled them back off.

Abe's mother looked at him and shook her head. He could tell she was not happy. He did not want her to look sad, but he did not want to go to school either.

"Did I ever tell you about another boy named Abe who wished he could go to school?" His mother sat down on the edge of his bed.

Abe sat up a little straighter. His mother sounded as though she was going to tell a story. He loved her stories.

"There was once a boy named Abe who wanted to learn, but sometimes he lived too far away to go to school."

Abe frowned. "Why wasn't he happy? He could sleep in late if he couldn't go to school."

Abe's mother laughed. "If he wasn't at school, he was working hard. He had to help his family, but he also wanted to help his family by learning as much as he could. Abe went to school whenever he could. He also studied at home. He read books that other people let him use. He even studied at night by the light of a candle because there was no electricity at his house."

"Who doesn't have electricity?" Abe asked his mother.

"Abraham Lincoln, that's who," his mother answered. "Little Abe grew up to become President Abraham Lincoln. He was one of the greatest presidents who ever lived. He believed you were lucky to get a good education. He could not have been such a great man if he hadn't wanted to learn."

Abe had learned a lot about President Lincoln in school. He knew he was a great man. He knew he loved his country. Abe made a decision. He slid out of his bed. "I want to grow up to be a great man like President Lincoln," Abe told his mother. "If the other Abe liked to learn, then so do I."

Abraham Lincoln

Most people have heard of Abraham Lincoln. Lincoln was president of the United States during the Civil War. But what do you know about Lincoln as a boy?

Abraham Lincoln was born in Kentucky in 1809. His first home was a log cabin. When he was two, his family moved. The family's new home was close to a trail that people took to move out West. Lincoln liked talking to all the people who traveled by his new home. He learned many things by talking to so many new people.

Lincoln also liked going to school. When he was at home, he would practice what he learned at school. When he was working outside, he would try to write his letters in the dirt and in the snow. He also learned from his parents. They would read out loud each night to the children as the family sat by a fire.

When Lincoln turned seven, his family moved again. They built a new cabin to live in. He had to work hard to help his father make their new home. When he could find time, he read many books that he borrowed from other people. Sometimes, he would carry a book with him to work outside in the fields. Whenever he had a break, he would read as much as he could. Some people thought he was lazy because he wanted to stop to read. They did not understand how much he loved to learn.

When Lincoln was older, he began studying books to become a lawyer. He learned as much as he could. He wanted to make a difference in the world. One day, all of his education helped him to become someone people will never forget. The little boy who wanted to read and learn became president of the United States of America.

The following pages have questions based on the texts from Unit 26. You may look at the stories to help answer any questions. Use the back of the page if you need extra space for writing your answers.

1 Which paragraph in the text "Abraham Lincoln" explains why some people thought Lincoln was lazy?

    (a) paragraph 1

    (b) paragraph 2

    (c) paragraph 3

    (d) paragraph 4

2 Why did Lincoln carry a book with him when he was working outside?

_____

_____

_____

3 In the story "The Lesson," what lesson does Abe learn?

    (a) that it's okay to sleep in late

    (b) that getting a good education is important

    (c) that there are lots of boys who have the same first name that he has

    (d) that he will be president when he is older

4 Which sentence best describes Abraham Lincoln as a boy?

    (a) He liked to play outside.

    (b) He liked to travel.

    (c) He liked to read and learn.

    (d) He liked to hunt and fish.

5 What do the two texts have in common?

    (a) They are both about Abraham Lincoln.

    (b) They are both about sleeping in late.

    (c) They are both about the Civil War.

    (d) They are both about reading books.

6 What important job does Abraham Lincoln have once he gets older?

(a) He becomes a farmer.

(b) He becomes president of the United States of America.

(c) He becomes a tour guide.

(d) He becomes a teacher.

7 Write the sentence from the text "Abraham Lincoln" that helped you to answer #6.

_____

_____

_____

8 Which event happened first in the story "The Lesson"?

(a) Abe decided to go to school.

(b) Abe's mother told him a story.

(c) Abe pulled the covers over his head.

(d) Abe remembered learning about President Lincoln in school.

9 Which is an effect of Abraham Lincoln reading books?

(a) He learned a lot.

(b) He had to get glasses.

(c) He never did any work.

(d) He became very lazy.

10 What will most likely happen the next time Abe's mother tries to wake him up for school?

(a) He will get up more quickly.

(b) He will hide under the covers.

(c) He will ask his mother for another story.

(d) He will tell her he does not want to go to school.

Time to Write!

President Abraham Lincoln used to wear a hat called a stovepipe hat. Look at the stovepipe hat below. Write sentences inside the hat explaining why all children should want to go to school and learn. Give at least three good reasons why it is important to go to school.

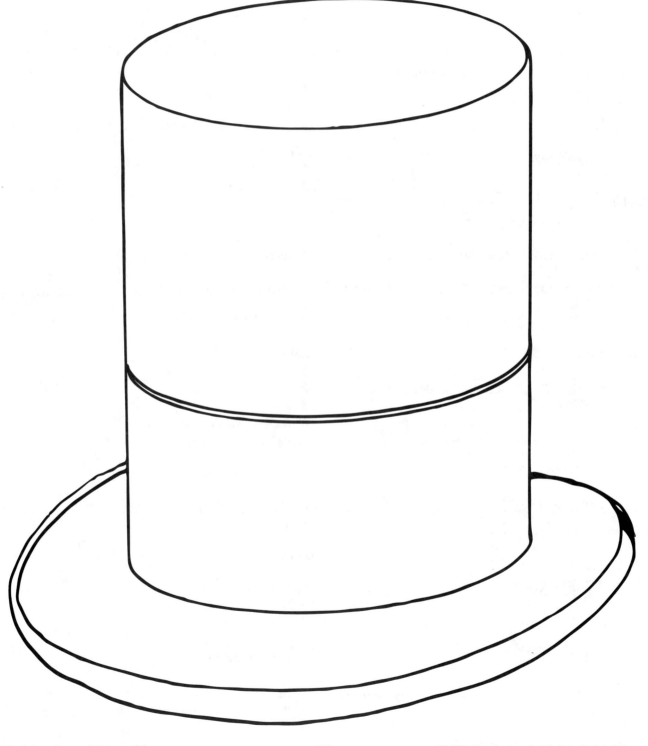

Answer Key

Unit 1
1. b
2. d
3. c
4. Answers will vary.
5. d
6. The stripes represent the original 13 colonies.
7. They are always traveling.
8.–10. Answers will vary.

Unit 2
1. a
2. a
3. a
4. Answers will vary but must explain the answer chosen for #3.
5. b
6.–7. Answers will vary.
8. b
9. Answers will vary.
10. safety pin

Unit 3
1. b
2. d
3. The other waterfall is in Canada.
4. ☺
5. Answers will vary but must show Candy is happy about the move.
6. c
7. a
8. a
9. b
10. Answers will vary but must show Candy likes new experiences.

Unit 4
1. b
2. c
3. d
4. "We don't want to leave anything out, or we might have some uninvited guests," Jesse's dad explained.
5. Answers will vary.
6. tent, backpack, motor home
7. backpack
8. Answers will vary.
9. b
10. a

Unit 5
1. d
2. d
3. He couldn't wait to have another chance to talk in front of the class.
4. a
5. Answers will vary.
6. a
7. a
8. c
9. b
10. Answers will vary.

Unit 6
1. c
2. b
3. Answers will vary.
4. b
5. The cactus is prickly and was a present.
6. a
7. b
8. Answers will vary.
9. b
10. The cactus will not do well or may even die.

Unit 7
1. c
2. Answers will vary.
3. b
4. Answers will vary.
5. d
6. Answers will vary.
7. b
8. He hoped the school would have another contest very soon.
9. a
10. Answers will vary.

Unit 8
1. d
2. d
3. a
4. Answers will vary.
5. He had been waiting for the weather to be perfect.
6. b
7. Answers will vary.
8. b
9. d
10. a

Unit 9
1. a
2. b
3. She was very scared.
4. b
5. b
6. Answers will vary.
7. d
8. He wants to start a sticker chart as a reward system.
9. It worked for him when he was afraid to go to the dentist.
10. b

Answer Key *(cont.)*

Unit 10
1. c
2. a
3. Answers will vary.
4. a
5. The hidden treasures are fossils. They are called "treasures" because they are special.
6. d
7. a
8. They can teach about the past.
9. Fossils can give us a lot of information. (or) Well-preserved fossils can show almost exactly what an animal or plant once looked like.
10. Students should circle the leaf imprint on the rock.

Unit 11
1. a
2. Answers will vary.
3. A legend is a story that some people believe is true even if there is no real evidence to prove the story is real.
4. d
5. b
6. **a.** He liked being able to see all the names of the cities and towns they were passing.

   b. He wanted to use the map to find the area where Bigfoot might be.
7. b
8. a, b, c
9. Answers may vary.
10. a

Unit 12
1. a
2. c
3. c
4. c
5. Catgut is part of the inside intestines of some animals such as sheep or goats.
6. c
7.–8. Answers will vary.
9. a
10. Sewing has been around for thousands of years.

Unit 13
1. Answers will vary.
2. b
3. Answers will vary.
4. b
5. c
6. b
7. a
8. He wanted to be able to do more for his family.
9. a
10. He was winning. (or) He had won first place!

Unit 14
1. c
2. d
3. Answers will vary.
4. b
5. the hoop
6.–7. Answers will vary.
8. d
9. b
10. d

Unit 15
1. b
2. c
3. d
4. Answers will vary.
5. b
6. d
7. c
8. c
9. b
10. She dug the spade into the dirt.

Unit 16
1. c
2. c
3. d
4. Long ago, people drew pictures on the walls of caves.
5. Both are about writing.
6. Answers will vary.
7. b
8. a
9. a
10. His mother says that being neat shows he cares about his work.

Unit 17
1. c
2.–3. Answers will vary.
4. Maddie and Mr. Jackson
5. b
6. d
7. a
8. c
9. Answers will vary.
10. No one ever interviews the teachers, yet they are a part of the school, too.

Unit 18
1. b
2. b
3. a
4. b
5. The word *suffrage* means the right to vote.

Answer Key (cont.)

6. a

7. At that moment, she was proud of her mother just for voting.

8. Answers will vary.

9. c

10. b

Unit 19

1. b

2. c

3. b, c, a

4. d

5. Halloween

6. d

7. "You forgot to say 'trick or treat' at your very first house!"

8. c

9. d

10. They would light huge bonfires to keep away evil spirits.

Unit 20

1. c

2. d

3. Bell invented the telephone.

4. Answers will vary.

5. d

6. a

7. **a.** air
   b. plane

8. b

9.–10. Answers will vary.

Unit 21

1. d

2. c

3. Anne Frank or Helen Keller

4. b

5. d

6. a

7. Answers will vary.

8. d

9. That night, Sophie wrote three pages in her diary.

10. a

Unit 22

1. d

2. c

3. b

4. c

5. Answers will vary.

6. c

7. b

8. b

9. b

10. They feed on other animals of the sea.

Unit 23

1. b

2. a

3. a

4. c

5. She did not want the girls to be angry with her.

6. c

7. a

8. a

9. b

10. Answers will vary.

Unit 24

1. d

2. a

3. Answers will vary.

4. b

5. People who have eaten insects say they often have a nutty taste.

6. b

7. Both texts are about eating things that are hard for some people to eat.

8. a

9. d

10. b

Unit 25

1. b

2. **a.** basket
   b. ball

3. a

4. b

5. c

6. b

7. c

8. In some countries, the game is called "football" instead of "soccer."

9. c

10. c

Unit 26

1. d

2. so he could read whenever he had a break

3. b

4. c

5. a

6. b

7. The little boy who wanted to read and learn became president of the United States of America.

8. c

9. a

10. a

Meeting Standards

Each passage and activity meets one or more of the following Common Core State Standards©
Copyright 2010. National Governors Association Center for Best Practices and Council of Chief State
School Officers. All rights reserved. For more information about the Common Core State Standards, go
to *http://www.corestandards.org/* or *http://www.teachercreated.com/standards/*.

Reading: Literature	Passages and Activities
Key Ideas and Details	
ELA.RL.3.1: Ask and answer questions to demonstrate understanding of a text, referring explicitly to the text as the basis for the answers.	All fiction
ELA.RL.3.3: Describe characters in a story (e.g., their traits, motivations, or feelings) and explain how their actions contribute to the sequence of events.	All fiction
Craft and Structure	
ELA.RL.3.4: Determine the meaning of words and phrases as they are used in a text, distinguishing literal from nonliteral language.	Unit 4, Unit 5, Unit 10, Unit 13
Range of Reading and Level of Text Complexity	
ELA.RL.3.10: By the end of the year, read and comprehend literature, including stories, dramas, and poetry, at the high end of the grades 2–3 text complexity band independently and proficiently.	All fiction
Reading: Informational Text	**Passages and Activities**
Key Ideas and Details	
ELA.RI.3.1: Ask and answer questions to demonstrate understanding of a text, referring explicitly to the text as the basis for the answers.	All nonfiction
ELA.RI.3.2: Determine the main idea of a text; recount the key details and explain how they support the main idea.	All nonfiction
Craft and Structure	
ELA.RI.3.4: Determine the meaning of general academic and domain-specific words and phrases in a text relevant to a *grade 3 topic or subject area*.	All nonfiction
Integration of Knowledge and Ideas	
ELA.RI.3.7: Use information gained from illustrations (e.g., maps, photographs) and the words in a text to demonstrate understanding of the text (e.g., where, when, why, and how key events occur).	All nonfiction
ELA.RI.3.8: Describe the logical connection between particular sentences and paragraphs in a text (e.g., comparison, cause/effect, first/second/third in a sequence).	All nonfiction
ELA.RI.3.9: Compare and contrast the most important points and key details presented in two texts on the same topic.	All units

Meeting Standards *(cont.)*

Range of Reading and Level of Text Complexity	
ELA.RI.3.10: By the end of the year, read and comprehend informational texts, including history/social studies, science, and technical texts, at the high end of the grades 2–3 text complexity band independently and proficiently.	All nonfiction
Writing	**Passages and Activities**
Text Types and Purposes	
ELA.W.3.1: Write opinion pieces on topics or texts, supporting a point of view with reasons.	Unit 2, Unit 18, Unit 23, Unit 26
ELA.W.3.2: Write informative/explanatory texts to examine a topic and convey ideas and information clearly.	Unit 9, Unit 11 , Unit 13, Unit 15, Unit 16, Unit 17, Unit 24, Unit 25
ELA.W.3.3: Write narratives to develop real or imagined experiences or events using effective technique, descriptive details, and clear event sequences.	Unit 3, Unit 4, Unit 7, Unit 8, Unit 11, Unit 12, Unit 19, Unit 21
Production and Distribution of Writing	
ELA.W.3.4: With guidance and support from adults, produce writing in which the development and organization are appropriate to task and purpose.	All units
ELA.W.3.5: With guidance and support from peers and adults, develop and strengthen writing as needed by planning, revising, and editing.	All units
ELA.W.3.6: With guidance and support from adults, use technology to produce and publish writing (using keyboarding skills) as well as to interact and collaborate with others.	All units
Research to Build and Present Knowledge	
ELA.W.3.7: Conduct short research projects that build knowledge about a topic.	Unit 1, Unit 5, Unit 6, Unit 10, Unit 14, Unit 22
ELA.W.3.8: Recall information from experiences or gather information from print and digital sources; take brief notes on sources and sort evidence into provided categories.	All units
Range of Writing	
ELA.W.3.10: Write routinely over extended time frames (time for research, reflection, and revision) and shorter time frames (a single sitting or a day or two) for a range of discipline-specific tasks, purposes, and audiences.	All units